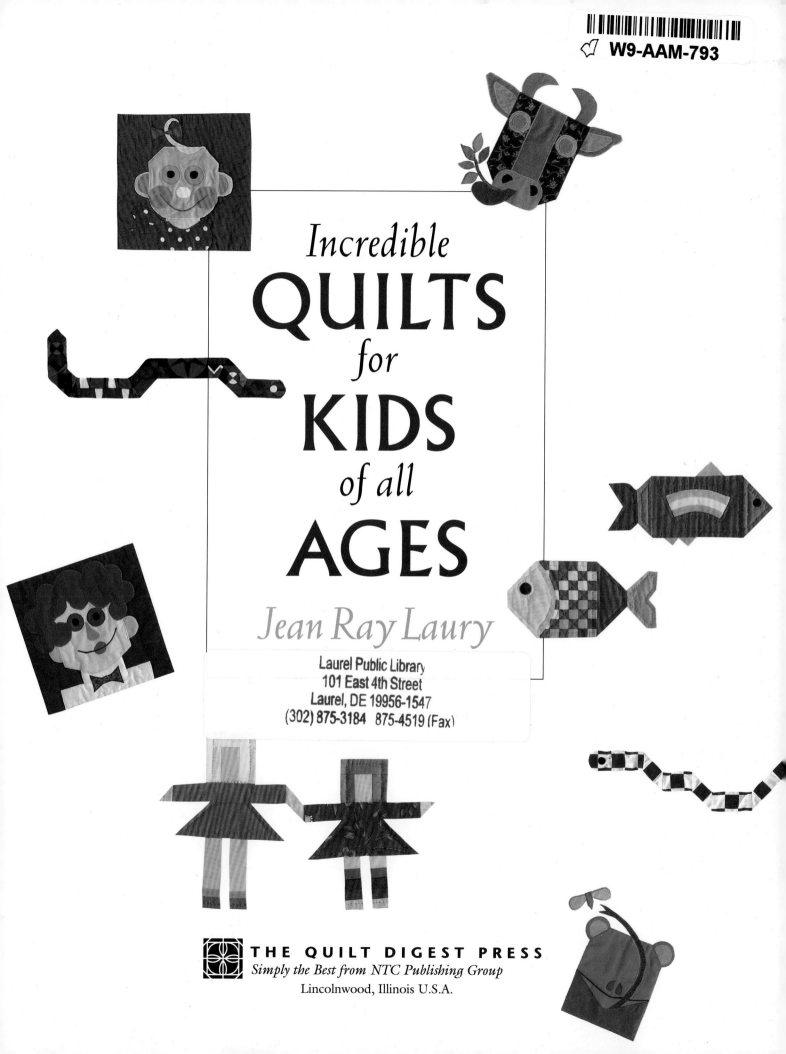

Incredible
QUILTS
for
KIDS
of all
AGES

Jean Ray Laury

THE QUILT DIGEST PRESS
Simply the Best from NTC Publishing Group
Lincolnwood, Illinois U.S.A.

Editorial and production direction by Bill Folk.

Production management by James Nelson.

Editing by Jan Johnson.

Technical editing by Kandy Peterson and Janet Reed.

Copyediting by Janet Reed.

Illustrations by Kandy Peterson.

Book and cover design by Kajun Graphics, San Francisco.

Photography by Sharon Risedorph, San Francisco.

Typographical composition by DC Typography, San Francisco.

Special thanks to Lynne Coenen for her support.

Second printing.

Cataloging-in-Publication Data is available from the Library of Congress.

1996 Printing

Published by The Quilt Digest Press, a division of NTC Publishing Group
4255 West Touhy Avenue, Lincolnwood (Chicago) Illinois 60646-1975 U.S.A.

6 7 8 9 0 WKT 0 9 8 7 6 5 4 3 2

When Michael Kile first asked me to do a book of quilts for children, I responded that I was past that stage of my life. He laughed and said that was only partly true. We talked about how quilts (or paintings or stories) for youngsters must exist on several levels. As children grow, additional layers of significance should become evident. This is why we never tire of reading *Alice in Wonderland* or *Winnie-the-Pooh*. Most adults can count at least one Eeyore among their acquaintances and probably a clock-watching Mad Hatter as well. We discussed the universal appeal of color, pattern, and humor, and of animals and people. We wanted visually exciting ideas for the kids and designs that would spark quilters' creativity.

I dedicate this book to the memory of Michael, who understood the importance of humor, play, and imagination.

ACKNOWLEDGMENTS

Designing these quilts was fun. After that the real work began, and I had expert help from an extraordinary group of quilting friends. It was a learning process for us all, as designs were added, changed, developed, or eliminated while we worked together. My warmest thanks to Cheryl Berman, Nancy Clemmensen, Judy DeRouchey, Ann Diebert, Carolyn Greer, Jody House, Bev Karau, Jean Sayeg, Marguerite Shattuck, Ruth Sherman, Bea Slater, Susan Smeltzer, and Joyce Smith.

The team at The Quilt Digest Press was a pleasure to work with, from our first meeting to the final color proofs. I especially wish to thank Jan Johnson and Janet Reed, who edited the text and deftly whisked away grammatical blunders; Kandy Petersen, for her fine drawings; Laurie Smith and Pat Koren, for their wonderful design; and Sharon Risedorf, for her superb photography.

Front row (l. to r.): Bev Karau, Bea Slater, Jody House, Jean Ray Laury, Cheryl Berman; Back row (l. to r.): Jean Sayeg (white sleeves), Susan Smeltzer, Marguerite Shattuck, Nancy Clemmensen, Ruth Sherman, Ann Diebert, Joyce Smith. Not pictured: Judy DeRouchey

CONTENTS

INTRODUCTION

If that's a baby quilt," asked five-year-old David, "what's it going to be when it grows up?"

The thought of a baby quilt as an infant of its species tickles our funny bones. We all know that the baby grows up; the quilt stays the same.

Or does it? Time plays games with our recollections. We exaggerate and magnify some memories so that they substantiate what we "know." Who isn't surprised, upon visiting a childhood home unseen for years, at how small the house is?

Quilts are among the treasured childhood possessions subject to exaggerated or distorted memories. One may be recalled as huge and fluffy because of the warmth, security, comfort, and satisfaction in which it wrapped the child. A quilting friend, whose mother sent her the faded and tattered quilt that had been the daughter's childhood favorite, denied ownership. She maintained, "This is not the same one." The one *she* recalled was huge and had thousands of bright colors. More than once, adult siblings have reverted to childish arguments about who a quilt really belonged to.

In their drawings, children illustrate the relative importance of things in several ways. One of these, the most telling and amusing, is in relative size. They may depict themselves prominently, and oversized, in the center of a page. Mother, especially if she is at home all day, may be drawn double the size of a less often seen father. Baby sister may appear as a small scribble in the corner or may simply not exist. (The total elimination of siblings is revealing!) Through drawings, a child expresses personal feelings as to the relative importance of family members. This child's-eye view may ignore the obvious fact that mother weighs 125 pounds to father's 250 pounds. Our attachments and what we see or are aware of informs what or who we value. This

affects how we remember childhood quilts. The lucky people who possessed them as children probably have wonderful memories about their particular quilts, whether or not they would actually recognize them now.

Ostensibly, we make quilts for kids because they need covers to keep them warm. But that's only the excuse. Our real reasons have to do with the symbolic and ceremonial values of these endearing covers. When we wrap children in quilts, we tell them how important they are. We announce that importance to ourselves, to family, and to friends. The quilt helps to welcome a child into his or her expanding world. Making a special quilt for a particular child is one small but important way in which we help to create that world.

Making quilts for kids makes *us* more playful. When we're quilting for kids, we can be less concerned with convention and tradition, and less confined. Giving full swing to a spontaneous, unrestricted exuberance is a joy.

A quilt may be loved into extinction after being hugged, tugged, and cuddled in for a dozen years. If you plan a masterpiece quilt that you envision will be admired for generations, save it for a wedding gift. A child's quilt *should* be used and enjoyed if it is to become an indelible part of the child's memories. Knowing our work will get slept on, spilled on, and dragged about, adds to our more playful approach. Kids' quilts will be draped over chairs to create tents and hideaways. They will get wrapped over shoulders to become robes for queens and capes for magicians. Making them expands and clarifies our ideas of what quilting is about.

Kids' quilts can reflect a child's current passion for cats, space, or airplanes. A quilt that reflects that passion sends positive signals, validating and adding importance to the child's pursuits. The beetles and snakes that an eight-year-old is crazy about are perfectly appropriate to a quilt, and they encourage the future entomologist or herpetologist as well.

In this book, the quilts *Fish, Creepy Crawlies,* and *Animal Fair* reflect some keen interests of youngsters. The *My Family* quilt offers a good example of how personal each of these covers can become. With simple color and design variations, the faces change and family portraits emerge: Dad with his square chin, Aunt Peggy with a mop of yellow hair, or Granny in her glasses. Any relative can be depicted from the versatile patterns. Every quilt made from these drawings will be one of a kind.

The best children's quilts are not just the result of making fewer full-sized blocks and assembling them into traditional patterns. When the total quilt size is smaller, a correspondingly smaller block will keep the proportions in scale. Kid's quilts are a different world in terms of subject matter, style, color, and size. In making them, we direct attention to images and content, to color and exuberance. Children respond to absorbing detail, stimulating colors, and humor. They thrive on designs that encourage their imaginations.

Making a kid's quilt every so often helps us maintain our perspective on what's really important in life. Entering this world, we tread in delicate territory. Children are unhesitating as critics. If they think brown is ugly, they won't mince words. They can get the full range of their opinions into one resounding *yuk*. But they offer their generous and heartfelt appreciation with equal enthusiasm. They'll often enjoy being consulted on some decisions. Offer five or six prints or colors that you find workable, and let the child select three favorites to include. Should this clown have a round nose or a triangular nose—or no nose at all? Should the yellow goose have red feet or orange feet? And what color socks are needed for little sister? This involvement helps short-circuit the possibility of yuks.

Be sure to sign and date your quilt. First in importance is the name of the quiltmaker. The inclusion of your relationship as aunt, mother, or grandmother will only add to the quilt's sentimental and personal value. The date is also important, and including the name of the child for whom you've made the quilt will solve differences of opinion and settle "that one was mine" arguments thirty years from now. Add the name of your town, too. Should your quilt actually survive the childhood for which it was made, family and quilt historians a few generations hence will be grateful for this extra bit of information.

This book is filled with new and original designs that will appeal to grown-ups as well as kids. They are a delight to use, fun to see, and a treat to make. Don't be too quick to decide how old a kid has to be to enjoy these designs. Lots of very large, mature kids (past forty) have expressed pointed interest in having one of these as their own.

Making quilts for kids should be fun. Relax about the quiltmaking. This is not necessarily the place for your most intricate piecing or finest stitches. Make a quilt with love and pleasure, and those qualities will accompany the quilt on its way. It'll be enjoyed and loved. For kids, loving something doesn't usually mean admiring it from a distance. Loving a quilt may mean sprawling on it to enjoy a peanut butter sandwich—or it may mean sharing its warmth with the dog. But the quilt will be used, and its daily use is a tribute to your success. Knowing that is part of making quilts for kids.

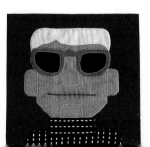

COLORS

The pleasures of kids' quilts are not only for the kids. For quilt-makers, going "all out" for the brightest and most appealing colors makes the project as much fun as the unconventional subject matter does.

Clear, pure, unadulterated colors, often thought of as childlike, are commonly used in the manufacture of kids' toys, furniture, and play clothes. And with good reason: Children are attached to the sunny colors. Beaming with brightness, these colors jump straight off the color wheel or fall right out of the rainbow. Even the youngest children respond to a whole spectrum of bright colors—including violets, greens, and yellows—not just to the pastel pinks and blues of traditional baby quilts.

In making your color choices, decide on the overall feeling you'd like your quilt to have: Quiet and restful? Active and wild? Warm and inviting? Produce the effect through color interaction. Close colors tend to create a more restful, cohesive, unified feeling. Colors that contrast, that are unalike, tend to be more active, to separate.

Most of us are comfortable with colors that relate or tie together in any of several ways. For example, they can be close in hue, as when we use a whole assortment of reds or blues together. We combine colors this way in our clothing, in our kitchens or living rooms. An outfit including a blue sweater, light blue turtleneck, and navy skirt offers an example.

Or colors can be similar in intensity, which refers to their dullness or brightness. Bright colors, those with high intensities, are simple and pure, and we expect to see them in a child's room. The colors we do *not* associate with children are the muted, muddied, mixed colors of lower intensities or dark, dense colors. These "heavy" colors are full of hidden and mysterious complexities and lack the fresh openness of the childlike brights. The rich, muted colors of fall are dull, low-intensity colors. Each starts out bright and is then muddied by the addition of its complement on the color wheel. Add a touch of green to red, and it turns brown. Add a bit of violet to yellow, and it goes dull.

Finally, colors can be related in value, as darks or lights. The addition of white to colors makes light values, or tints, which tend to be more soothing, quiet, and soft instead of energetic, lively, and bright. These light or pastel colors are often associated with younger children and account for the pale pinks and soft greens of baby clothes. The addition of black to colors makes them dark values, or shades. Prints often combine a variety of light or dark values.

When colors contrast, or when they do not share common characteristics, they are more noticeable and more active. They demand more attention, and they are harder to handle. If you feel uncertain or hesitant about color use, start with colors related in one of the ways just described. With more experience and confidence, you'll try greater contrasts.

Quilts reflect all sorts of ways of combining colors. Amish quilts contain many close colors, usually dark and intense. Pennsylvania Dutch quilts are often full of brights, including reds, yellows, and greens. Baby quilts appear in pale, soft pastels. Kids' quilts use clear and bright colors of high intensity. Quilts with lots of contrast, such as those made by Katie Pasquini, Yvonne Porcella, or Nancy Crow are active, dynamic, and energetic. Many quilts from the thirties, made with soft, muted pinks, pale greens, and dusty blues, are comparatively quiet.

Most of the quilts offered here use solid-colored fabrics to set off bright prints, stripes, or polka dots. The combination yields striking color results. A quilt with too little contrast may seem dull. Too much contrast may be frenetic.

In *Circus Clowns*, clear, bright colors are combined with strong contrasts of red and white. It is a quilt full of energy, and one that might keep most of us awake. The dancing polka dots and stripes may get your rods and cones overexcited. The *Big Brother/Little Sister* quilt is made up of softer, subtler, quieter colors. When we juxtapose darks and lights or dulls and brights, we create contrasts, and these contrasts offer the most powerful color effects.

Printed fabrics offer wonderful small-scale patterns and variations within block parts. When selecting prints, be sure to view them from a few feet away as well as up close. At a distance, colors blend, as in an Impressionist painting. Blue and yellow lines, easily visible when seen up close, will blend into green when seen from farther away. A tiny red-on-white polka dot will appear as pink from a distance; the fragmented bits of color, the red dots, will have less impact than the impression of pink.

Look at prints in terms of dark or light value. The overall value will be the factor that most affects how any print works. For example, in *Big Sister/Little Sister*, it would be difficult to use dark prints for the girls because the background is a black print. Even tiny white flowers and green leaves on a dark ground would be lost against that black print. Contrast allows the figure to show up, so light and bright colors work best.

Because certain colors are in fashion each year, we don't always have a full range of choices. One year you may find magentas everywhere, and the next year tangerine may dominate. Just don't try to locate tangerine during a magenta year! Because of these constant changes in color availability, maintaining a fabric stash is critical. By gathering colors from year to year, we accumulate a wide-ranging, full palette. And we need this collection of colors from which to make selections in the same way that a painter needs tubes of paints of many hues. A cluster of five different reds creates a stronger impression than will any single red. It's like having a string of adjectives to describe something or using a variety of herbs in your cooking. Trading swatches of fabric with other quilters expands your color palette.

One of the reasons we all like to make children's quilts is because we feel free of any obligation to make "good" color combinations. We can do what we like and what we know kids will like. It means choosing exciting, joyful, stimulating colors that we might otherwise shy away from as too bright or gaudy. There is no need, in making quilts for children, to select subdued, sober, or safe colors that "go" with the rest of a house. It is an exhilarating way to work, freed from our notions of how quilts "ought" to be.

FABRIC CHOICE

Selecting 100 percent cotton fabrics for your quilt will give the best results, including the smoothest seams. When you mix fibers and sew a cotton to a cotton blend, the seamline is rarely entirely smooth or free from tiny ripples. But the benefits of using cotton are most evident in the quilting. The natural fiber of cotton is more flexible, forgiving, and pliable. It's easier to quilt, and the stitches look better than they do over a synthetic or a blend.

Children especially enjoy the softness of cotton fabric. It feels good next to the skin, and its softness increases with wear and washing.

Some of the brilliant colors in blended fabrics cannot be duplicated in cotton. Those bright colors are inviting, but in selecting them you compromise on other aspects of the quilt. Blends have the advantage of nonwrinkling finishes, but, once stained, they are difficult to bring back to their original color.

Always purchase the best cotton fabrics you can afford. The advantages in terms of wear and longevity offset the increased cost. The primary expense of any quilt is in the time and energy invested in it, so reward your efforts with high-quality cloth.

While it's nice to have fresh, new fabric, it doesn't have to be newly purchased. Garage sales and thrift shops may yield unusual fabrics no longer available. Check with family and friends for fabric scraps, as many are delighted to see their remnants recycled. And trade with quilting friends. Always wash and press all fabrics to avoid any problems of colorfastness or shrinkage. You may need to supplement your collection by buying fabrics for borders, though they can be pieced or multicolored, too. You can make the back of your quilt from bands or large squares of color, rather than a single color.

Many of the quilts in this book are scrap quilts. They offer the perfect opportunity to sew up the treasured remnants squirreled away in boxes, cupboards, and drawers. Plan your quilt, purchase the yardage, and then use your scraps to provide a freewheeling assortment of colors, prints, stripes, or plaids to complement the dominant colors. *Big Sister/ Little Sister* includes scraps of fabric collected from friends as well as from the depths of the sewing basket. *Goosie Goosie Gander* exhibits a glorious range of yellows and oranges that are surely scraps. Where would you find that many oranges in one shop? The *My Family, Big Brother/Little Brother,* and *Animal Fair* quilts all rely heavily on scrap for variation. However, each could be made from planned colors to fit the color scheme of a room.

Discovering just the right print among your scraps takes time, but it's fun. A tiny pattern may give a mossy look to the deer's antlers in *Animal Fair. Creepy Crawlies* invites the use of wild prints and linear patterns. Enhance the big sisters' dresses with patterns that help create sleeves and yokes and borders. On each, the scale of the print must relate to the size of the template. Take your transparent templates with you when you go to the fabric shop, and place them on top of prints. You can readily determine which will work. Do the same as you go through your scrap box. It's easy to fall in love with a fabric because of a sweet little lamb or doggy printed on it. But remember, the cute little thing may have its head unceremoniously snipped off before it gets sewn in.

Check prints for directional patterns, especially when cutting straight pieces for bindings, borders, or sashings. What appears to be an allover floral print, for instance, may have a repeat design that shows up as a line when it's in the quilt. This is especially distracting in

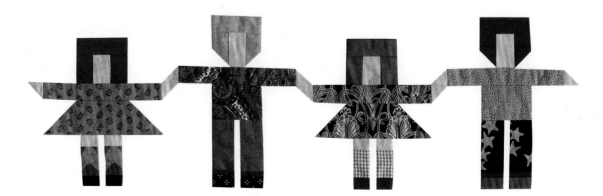

narrow bindings, where a print can create an effect of meandering or wavering lines. Select fabrics with directional patterns for specific uses. An obvious example is the striped binding on *Circus Clowns.*

To check the directional design of a print, unroll a couple of yards from the bolt and take a look at the design from a distance of 8 or 10 feet (about 3 m) or from an angle. The directional design will make a definite line. It is sometimes possible to specifically utilize those designs if they are midsized, from 1″ to 3″ (2.5 cm to 7.6 cm) across. The *Big Brother/Little Brother* quilt has a direction print used in one of the borders. Because the print is midsize to large scale (certainly not a tiny print), it produces a nice repeat design. In large-scale prints, directional lines are often less apparent once the fabric is cut into small or narrow pieces. To check, place two sheets of white paper on the fabric about 2″ (5.1 cm) apart. You will be able to see in the exposed area just how the pattern will look when used in the quilt.

DETERMINING SIZE

A quilt made to amuse and comfort a child can be just about any size or proportion. When the kid (of any age) nestles into a quilt on the sofa, the specific size matters little. Favorite quilts seldom see the top of a bed. But for those who prefer to have a quilt fit as a bed cover, here are some basic bed sizes.

Crib: 23″ × 46″ (58.4 cm × 116.8 cm)
Six-year crib: 27″ × 52″ (68.6 cm × 132.1 cm)
Youth bed: 33″ × 66″ (83.8 cm × 167.6 cm)
Twin bed: 39″ × 75″ (99.1 cm × 190.5 cm)
Long twin bed: 39″ × 80″ (99.1 cm × 203.2 cm)
Bunk bed: 38″ × 75″ (96.5 cm × 190.5 cm)
Wide single bed: 48″ × 75″ (121.9 cm × 190.5 cm)

Remember that any size quilt can cover the bed top if another cover drops over the mattress at the sides and foot of the bed. Try the quilt on the bed. If it covers the sides of the mattress, just add a dust ruffle. If the quilt is just a few inches larger than the bed top, use a cover that drops down the sides to within several inches of the floor. This offers great flexibility in the size of the quilt.

If you wish to extend the drop at the sides and bottom of a quilt, add 6″ to 8″ (15 cm to 20 cm) to each side and the bottom edge. If you wish the quilt to go to the floor, you will need a drop of 20″ to 21″ (51 cm to 53 cm). Wheels or coasters affect the bed height as do non-standard mattresses. Measure the bed for which you are planning the quilt. The terms *twin* or *single* are often used interchangeably in spite of their size differences.

If you want the quilt to cover pillows, that takes an extra 8″ to 10″ (20 cm to 25 cm) in length. If the quilt doesn't cover the pillows, you can use pillow shams, toss pillows, or pillowcases that blend.

Most of the quilts in this book can be readily adjusted in size. Obviously, if a quilt is made up from blocks, it is simply a matter of making more blocks for additional or wider rows, or fewer blocks for fewer rows. Quilts can be enlarged through the addition of borders or by widening sashing strips. In changing borders, it is a good idea to keep the measurements proportionate. That is, if borders given are 2″, 1″, and 3″ (5.1 cm, 2.5 cm, and 7.6 cm), enlarging them to 3″, 1½″, and 4½″ (7.6 cm, 3.8 cm, and 11.4 cm) would increase each by 50 percent and add 6″ (15.2 cm) to the width of the quilt. But the proportionate look would remain the same.

Changing the scale of a block is more difficult. All of the pieces must change in size and change proportionately. (It would be simpler to make additional blocks.) Read About Templates and Making Copies for further details on changing scale.

When you make changes in the blocks, remember the sashings and borders need to be adjusted accordingly. Either finish the blocks of a quilt first, then measure to determine border requirements, or draw out the new dimensions before starting, and figure your yardage and sizes all at once.

If you are fairly new to quilting, select a pattern that is already of an appropriate size. Old hands at quilting will be able to shift sizes with greater ease.

ABOUT TEMPLATES AND MAKING COPIES

To simplify your pattern cutting, make a set of templates for each block or design you intend to repeat. Our templates have been printed in strong clear black lines so that they can be easily traced. Using a translucent ¼″ (6 mm) scale graph paper will simplify the job. The grid provides an easy guide to check measurements and symmetrical shapes. Cut out all templates on the solid line. Sew on the broken line, or seamline. It is essential that cutting and sewing be accurate, especially on blocks that have many complex shapes.

You may wish to transfer your graph-paper template to a more rigid material, such as a translucent template grid. This will enable you to make exact copies, with the grid assuring accuracy. While most quilt shops carry some form of easy-to-use template material, you *can* make do (as your great grandmother did) with the cardboard from a box of cereal.

If you make copy-machine duplicates of the patterns, remember that some copiers distort the images slightly. For small appliqué shapes, the difference probably won't be enough to matter. On pieced patterns, however, always compare copies with the original and correct any differences.

Some copy machines enlarge by percentage while others have only a single enlargement option. Check local copy shops, blue printers, or drafting suppliers to locate a copier that can enlarge your block pattern to the specific size you need. Then make up your templates from that. Verify the accuracy with the original.

A small enlargement of an individual block will greatly enlarge the size of the quilt top. If there are ten blocks across the quilt, increasing a block by just 1½" (3.8 cm) enlarges a quilt by 15" (38 cm).

Always make up a sample block to check that the finished size (your block less seam allowance) is the same as the pattern. This gives you, in addition, a good test of your color and fabric. It is time and effort wisely invested.

Note that all templates include a ¼" (6 mm) seam allowance, except for pieces to be machine appliquéd. If you take a smaller or larger seam than this, you will need to adjust your templates accordingly.

Many pattern parts—for example, sashings and borders—are given in dimensions only. For these, use a rotary cutter or mark and cut with scissors. Templates are given for small shapes needed in multiples and for nongeometric shapes that cannot be easily described by measurement alone.

R ead this checklist before buying fabric, cutting patterns, or assembling your quilt.

1. Read through *all* the directions for a quilt before beginning any work.

2. Yardage requirements (provided in the directions for each quilt) are based on 45" (114.3 cm) wide fabric. They do not allow for straightening fabrics (if they are off grain or cut crooked) or for shrinkage, as this varies from one fabric to another. Buy enough extra so you're sure to have the required yardage after prewashing.

3. Rinse and iron dry any pearl cotton or cording and any nonwoven suedelike fabric to avoid problems of shrinkage or running.

4. Fabrics must be free of folds or wrinkles before pattern parts are cut.

5. All measurements include a ¼" (6 mm) seam allowance unless otherwise noted.

6. Unless otherwise directed, cut quilt parts for longer and larger pieces first. Then fit the smaller ones into the remaining fabric.

7. Sashings, borders, and bindings are cut on the lengthwise grain unless the cutting directions state otherwise.

8. All long sashings (excluding short ones between blocks) have 2" (5.1 cm) of excess fabric allowed in the lengths. This compensates for any variations in seam widths and assures ample length. Trim after sewing.

9. Use dark threads when sewing dark fabrics, light threads on light fabrics. High-quality thread will eliminate the frustration of shredded, frayed, and broken strands. When in doubt about the most appropriate color, choose the darker one.

10. Press seams to the side frequently as you assemble the quilt top. It is important that each seam be pressed before another piece is added.

11. To center an appliqué design on a block, fold both the appliqué piece and the block in quarters and crease. Stack appliqué on block and align folds.

BROTHERS AND SISTERS

All children who have even *heard* of Cinderella know about sibling rivalry. The presence of brothers or sisters means they probably experienced it before they could say either *Cinderella* or *sibling*. Most such rivalries don't involve a ball gown, glass slippers, or a handsome prince. More likely, they provide the newcomer with a tentative poke or a sly pinch (or, as in the movies, a high-speed ride in the perambulator). The fear that one sibling will usurp the position of another is a universal one, found in ancient myths, biblical stories, legends, folk tales, and most families.

The inclusion of an older brother or sister in the design of a quilt for a younger one may help forestall, or at least minimize, any feelings of being left out. Better yet, make the quilt for the older sibling. Strategies like this can smooth the often turbulent waters of coexistence.

Our specially designed figures of boys and girls can be arranged in a variety of ways. There are big and little sisters as well as big and little brothers. You can mix or match to customize your design.

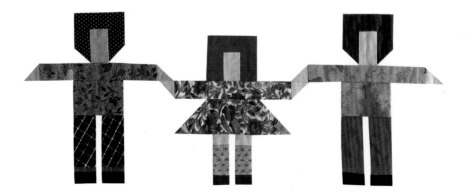

Children love watching these figures multiply, especially the images of themselves! Use prints and patterns from outgrown shirts to help a big brother identify himself in the quilt. Hair and skin color as well as dress patterns made from scraps of her outgrown clothes help assure an older sister that she has been singled out for a special spot.

Your color selections will determine the extent to which the figures will contrast or stand out. With a dark background, like the black print in *Big Sister/Little Sister* (see page 20), bright and light colors make a distinct contrast. The effect is lively and spirited, and the figures seem to dance across the quilt. Where the values of the colors are closer, and there is less contrast, as in *Big Brother/Little Sister* (see page 38), the effect is softer, quieter, and more restful.

The blocks are designed so that each figure has two hands—one of his or her own and one belonging to a sibling—on the right side. Hands are omitted on the left side, but when the big and little kids are assembled, the figures end up holding hands.

Because the end figures of each row join hands with only one sibling, instead of one on each side, "alternate" end blocks are necessary. These blocks use most of the regular templates but substitute a couple of alternate pieces to make it easy to replace the adjoining sibling's hand with background material. Alternate block templates are marked "a." See pages 22–23 for sample block and alternate block diagrams.

While our quilts include a variety of skin colors, selecting just two or three will simplify arranging for each figure to have two hands of identical color. To really simplify the assembly, choose a single skin color, and then all hands will match.

VARIATIONS OF BROTHER AND SISTER QUILTS

Should you prefer to use a single figure, rather than the pairs we have shown, make each block using all of the alternate templates (left and right). Add *one* hand at *each* side. Then the tips of the fingers will touch as the blocks are joined, or each block can be sashed individually.

Obviously, any combination of these figures can be used to make up a quilt: For example, you can connect a big sister with two little brothers. Since the hands appear to clasp only when one figure is taller than the other, alternating sizes are required if you want your kids to hold hands. You can make three hand-holding figures in a unit—the tall one in the center with the two shorter ones on the sides, or the reverse, with the short one in the center. Then use sashing around each unit. You'll be able to improvise once you become familiar with the pattern.

You might want to make a whole family, sewing parents into one row and children in the next. The row depicting parents could use blocks that have been lengthened (just add an inch or more to the legs and adjoining pieces). For a larger family, you could stair-step the children, having a taller one always clasping the hand of a shorter one. Start by making up a figure according to our pattern, and then try variations. As these variations change the size and proportion of the quilt, you will need to adjust the borders accordingly.

Use these block designs as a starting point and let your imagination take off. Don't forget that by changing hair and skin color you can personalize the figures. You might depict the children of your family with all their cousins or sew the members of a dance class or a scout troop.

A *Daddy Long Legs* quilt, with gangly long-legged kids, would require only the lengthening of the leg section in the boys' patterns. Any kid undergoing a growth spurt would enjoy some long-legged figures. Customizing your design will take some calculation on your part, but you will develop some wonderful variations from our basic kids.

This design is not limited to kids, of course. With a little shift in size, you can readily depict adults. Why not portray your quilting circle, showing them in their favorite getups? Your office mates or your in-laws are all fair game.

Directions follow and templates are at the back of the book. Note that although a few pattern parts are interchangeable, it will be simplest to make up a separate template for each.

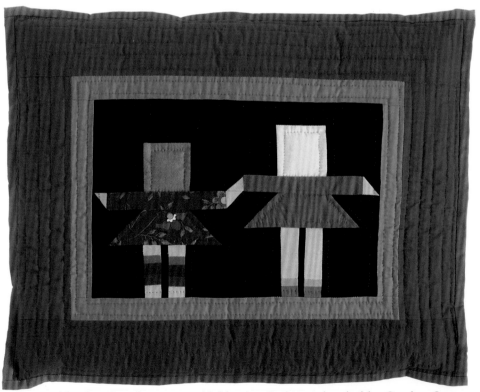

Designed by Jean Ray Laury, assembled by Ann Diebert and quilted by Carolyn Greer

BIG SISTER/ LITTLE SISTER

Who can resist this row-upon-row collection of little girls all decked out in polka dots and prints? Children of all ages respond to them, including those little girls about to leave for college! You can send your daughter away to school with a bevy of chums to keep her company.

This quilt can be adapted for Grown-Up Girls, too. How about a collection of nurses and doctors, all in white? Little white aprons would identify waitresses, and safari clothes would suggest anthropologists off on a field study. Any occupation may offer inspiration for a unique quilt that will never exist if you don't make it.

Little girls enjoy the addition of tiny details. Try some pockets with bits of lace for hankies. Appliqué skirts, aprons, or pinafores over the pieced dresses. Embroider bracelets, or tie tiny hair ribbons and stitch them in place. Once your blocks are made, the embellishing (which is the most fun) begins. Here is the perfect opportunity to use scraps from those favorite pajamas or prints from outgrown shirts or dresses to personalize the figures.

Hand-holding sisters pose and show off their new dresses for the photograph on page 20.

Read Before Starting Your Quilt on page 15.

Finished size: 41¾″ × 59½″ (106 cm × 151.1 cm)
Finished size of blocks and alternate right blocks: 6″ × 8½″
(15.2 cm × 21.6 cm)
Finished size of alternate left blocks: 6¾″ × 8½″
(17.1 cm × 21.6 cm)
Number of blocks: 25
Blocks set: 5 × 5

Designed by Jean Ray Laury, assembled by Ann Diebert and quilted by Carolyn Greer

YARDAGE

This is a perfect quilt for those favorite fabrics that you've had stashed away for years. Remember that these requirements are based on the use of single colors. When using assorted colors, allow a little more fabric as the cutting will be less efficient.

Background (black print): 1¼ yards (114 cm)
Figures (assorted colors)
    Hair: ¼ yard (23 cm)
    Face, hands, legs: ⅓ yard (31 cm)
    Dresses, socks: 1 yard (91 cm)
    Note: You may wish to use a striped fabric to suggest shoes and
    socks to avoid having to piece several colors together.
Sashing and first border (green): 1½ yards (137 cm)
Second border (blue): 1½ yards (137 cm)
Backing: 2⅔ yards (244 cm)
Batting: 46″ × 64″ (116.8 cm × 162.6 cm)
Binding (violet): ¾ yard (68.6 cm)

CUTTING

The diagrams show how the blocks are assembled and identify the pattern pieces. Templates are given for all pieces in the back of the book. Read all directions before beginning. An excess of about 2″ (5.1 cm) is allowed on all long sashing and border strips, to be trimmed after sewing.

13 Big sister blocks

A, O	26 each
B, C, D, F, G, K, P, Q	13 each
E, J, L, M, N	10 each
H, I	16 each
Ea, Ja, La, Na	3 each

12 Little sister blocks

A, O	24 each
B, C, D, G, K, L, M, P, Q	12 each
E, F, I, J, N	10 each
H	14
I	2 (in background color)
Ea, Fa, Ja, Na	2 each

Sashing and first border (green)
    Sashing strips: 4—33″ × 2″ (83.8 cm × 5.1 cm)
    Side border: 2—50″ × 2″ (127 cm × 5.1 cm)
    Top and bottom border: 2—36″ × 2″ (91.4 cm × 5.1 cm)

Second border (blue)
     Sides: 2—54″ × 4″ (134.2 cm × 10.2 cm)
      Top and bottom: 2—44″ × 4″ (111.8 cm × 10.2 cm)
Backing: 2—46″ (116.8 cm) lengths
Batting: 46″ × 64″ (116.8 cm × 162.6 cm)
Binding (violet): 8—2½″ (6.4 cm) strips × width of fabric

CONSTRUCTING THE BLOCKS

Read all directions before starting. Keep a diagram or picture of the sister blocks on hand to guide you in assembling the blocks.

If you use a single skin color for both sizes of sisters, you'll find assembly greatly simplified. Just complete all blocks as you go.

If you use two skin colors, one for each of the two sister sizes, then you must use the big sister hand color in the little sister blocks where the hands join. The reverse will be true in the big sister blocks. If you choose to work with a variety of skin colors, leave the hand seams open until you determine the final block placement. Then you can insert hand colors to match the adjoining faces.

To keep yourself sane, avoid mixing the sisters' templates.

Press the seams to the side as you go. For example, after joining A, B, and A (step 1), press seams carefully before you add C and D. Any seam that will be crossed with another piece should be firmly pressed first.

BIG SISTER BLOCKS

Make all big sister blocks first. Keep a diagram or picture of the block on hand to guide your assembly. The adjoining hand on the right side of each block will be in the little sister's skin color.

  1. Head section. Join A (hair), B (face), and A according to the diagram.
  2. Add C (hair), then D (background). Add backgrounds E and F.
  3. Arm section. Join H (hand) to I (background); add to G (arm).
  4. Skirt section. Join M (little sister's hand) to L (background). Then join J (background) to K (skirt) to L.
  5. Join head section to arm and skirt sections.
  6. Leg section. Join N (background), O (leg), P (background), O, and Q (background) in that order. *Note:* For part O (leg), piece fabrics to suggest socks and shoes or used striped materials to create the effect.

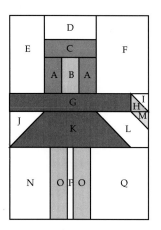

Big Sister Block
Make 7

Step 1

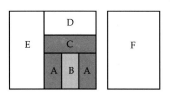

Step 2

Step 3

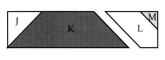

Step 4

7. Add leg section to skirt to complete the block.

8. When you complete your first big sister block, let the older sibling show it to friends and family, leaving no doubt about whose portrait has been made. Scraps of her own clothing will verify the identity.

Repeat steps 1–7 to make a total of seven big sister blocks. Then make the alternate blocks as follows:

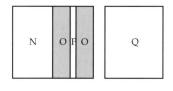

Step 5

BIG SISTER ALTERNATE LEFT BLOCKS

Follow steps 1–7 for making a big sister block, substituting parts Ea, Ja, and Na for parts E, J, and N and adding another I and H as shown in the diagram. You will now have a big sister with both a left and right hand as well as a connecting sibling's hand.

Repeat to make a total of three big sister alternate left blocks. You will use these on the left edge of rows 1, 3, and 5.

Step 6

BIG SISTER ALTERNATE RIGHT BLOCKS

Follow steps 1–7 for making a big sister block, this time substituting part La for parts L and M. You will have a big sister with only one hand and no connecting sibling's hand.

Repeat to make a total of three big sister alternate right blocks. You will use these on the right edge of rows 1, 3, and 5.

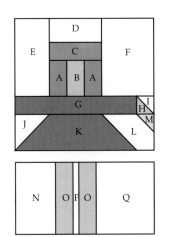

Step 7

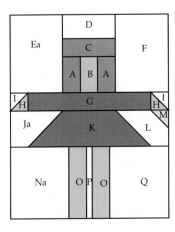

Big Sister Alternate Left
Make 3

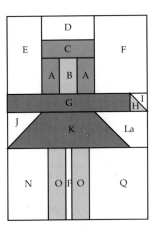

Big Sister Alternate Right
Make 3

LITTLE SISTER BLOCKS

Assembly for little sister is similar to that for big sister. The adjoining hand on the right side of each block (I) will be in the big sister's skin color.

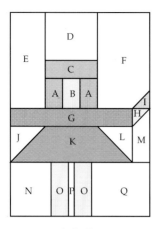

Little Sister
Make 8

1. Head section. Join A (hair), B (face), and A according to the diagram. Add C (hair) and D (background).
2. Add I (big sister's hand) to F (background). Then join backgrounds E and F to head section.
3. Dress section. Join backgrounds J and L to K (skirt) to make dress. Add G (sleeves) as shown.
4. Join H (hand) and M (background) and add to right end of sleeve and dress section, matching seams.
5. Add head section to dress section.
6. Leg section. Join N (background), O (leg), P (background), O, and Q (background) in that order. *Note:* For part O (leg), piece fabrics to suggest legs, socks, and shoes or use striped materials to create the same effect.
7. Add leg section to the rest to finish the block.

Repeat steps 1–7 to make a total of eight little sister blocks. Then make the alternate blocks as follows:

LITTLE SISTER ALTERNATE LEFT BLOCKS

Follow steps 1–7 for making a little sister block, substituting parts Ea, Ja, and Na for parts E, J, and N. Add another H and I as shown in the diagram. You will now have a little sister with both left and right hands as well as a connecting sibling's hand.

Repeat to make a second little sister alternate left block. You will use these on the left edge of rows 2 and 4.

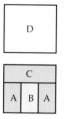

Step 1

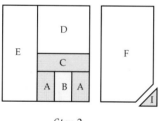

Step 2

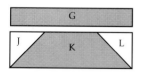

Step 3

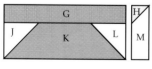

Step 4

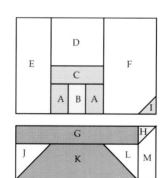

Step 5

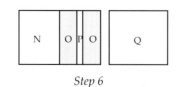

Step 6

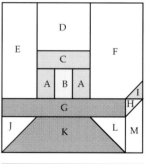

Step 7

24

LITTLE SISTER ALTERNATE RIGHT BLOCKS

Follow steps 1–7 for making a little sister block, this time substituting part Fa for parts F and I. You will have a little sister with only one hand and no connecting sibling's hand.

Repeat to make a second little sister alternate right block. You will use these on the right edge of rows 2 and 4.

ASSEMBLING THE QUILT TOP

1. Lay out the blocks, alternating big and little sisters, to determine the final arrangement. You will have 5 rows of 5 blocks each for a total of 25 blocks. Use the diagram as a guide, noting where alternate blocks fall. If you have not already done so, insert the proper hand colors in each block and close those final seams.

2. Join the completed sister blocks into 5 horizontal rows. Measure and sew carefully to assure that the rows are identical in width. Press. Measure a finished row, and then mark the same length on a green sashing strip. Pin them together at each end and at intervals between and sew. Continue so that the 5 rows of blocks are connected by 4 green sashing strips. Trim the ends of the sashing strips flush with the edges of the blocks. Press.

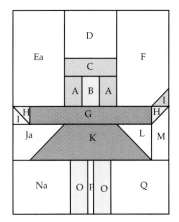

Little Sister Alternate Left
Make 2

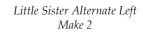

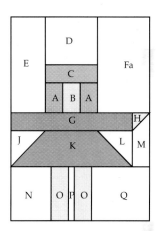

Little Sister Alternate Right
Make 2

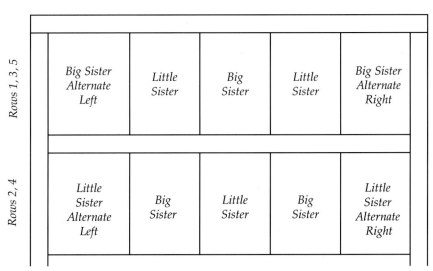

Assembly Diagram

Big Sister Alternate Left	*Little Sister*	*Big Sister*	*Little Sister*	*Big Sister Alternate Right*
Little Sister Alternate Left	*Big Sister*	*Little Sister*	*Big Sister*	*Little Sister Alternate Right*

Rows 1, 3, 5
Rows 2, 4

ADDING BORDERS

1. Add the longer green borders to the sides of the quilt top, again measuring and pinning. Sew and press.

2. Add the remaining green borders at the top and bottom, as above. Let these borders overlap the side borders to create a solid corner of green. Trim and press.

3. Add the second, blue borders to the sides of the quilt. Trim ends.

4. Then add the remaining blue borders to the top and bottom edges, again overlapping to create a solid corner. Trim and press.

BACKING

Since this quilt finishes at 41¾″ (106 cm) wide, it is possible to use a 45″ (114.3 cm) fabric for the width of the backing. This leaves little excess for the quilting but does avoid having any seams on the back. If you prefer to have a more ample backing, join 2 lengths of fabric, each 46″ (116.8 cm) long, on the lengthwise grain after cutting away selvages. Shift the seamline toward one end so that the excess is in a single large piece rather than in two smaller ones. Trim so that 2″ to 3″ (5.1 cm to 7.6 cm) of excess fabric remains on each edge. This will give you one horizontal seam across the back.

QUILTING

Read the sections on batting, layering, and quilting on pages 116–120 at the end of this book.

Spread out the quilt backing; cover it with batting and the quilt top. Our quilt is hand quilted with a medium blue quilting thread. Quilt ¼″ (6 mm) from the seamlines, going through all the layers. Start with the sashings and the green borders. Then quilt the blue borders. Finally, quilt around each of the individual figures.

BINDING

The violet color used throughout the figures is picked up in the binding color. Join the binding strips with diagonal seams. Follow our general directions for binding given on page 120. This quilt binding has squared, overlapped corners and finishes at ½″ (13 mm).

THE FINAL TOUCH

When you sign and date this quilt, it might be a good idea to include the name of the quilt owner. It'll preclude arguments years down the road when siblings, taking proprietary interest, each specifically recalls owning the quilt. It might, in fact, be a good idea to just plan on making two quilts to start with. Read about signing on page 123 of this book.

MAKING BIG SISTER / LITTLE SISTER PILLOWS

A few extra sisters have taken up residence on pillows. These whimsical pillows are certainly easier to tug about than an entire quilt. And since this quilt is a great favorite with children, pillows offer a simple solution to sharing.

We've made two pillows, each with two sister panels. On one, the sisters face away—the backs of their heads are suggested by omitting the faces and substituting hair color (see page 18).

Add sashing and borders to the panels as on the quilt, varying widths according to your pillow size. Once you have determined your pillow size, you will need (for each pillow) a rectangle of the same size to back the quilting as well as a panel to back the pillow.

Place a finished pillow top over batting and backing, then quilt, using a pattern similar to what is used on the quilt. Trim edges.

To finish the pillow, first sew binding to one short end of the pillow top in the same way you would sew binding on a quilt. Sew it to the front, but do not hand stitch it to the back. Place the pillow top face up on the wrong side of the rectangle that will back the pillow. When you sew the binding to the other three edges of the pillow top, also sew through this panel. Insert a pillow into the open end, and slip stitch the binding to the back of the pillow on all four sides.

Make a show of presenting the pillow to its new owner.

Designed by Jean Ray Laury, assembled by Ann Diebert and quilted by Carolyn Greer

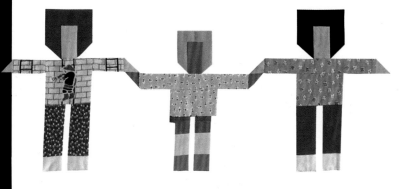

BIG BROTHER / LITTLE BROTHER

These brothers, all lined up for "crack the whip" or "tug-of-war," are irresistible. Long pants definitely distinguish the older boy from his younger brother in short pants, as does a size difference. You can put them all in long pants to make them older and to avoid the piecing of several small parts. Or put them all in short pants to suggest preschoolers.

Salvaged fabric scraps from outgrown clothes will blend right into this potpourri of color. The rainbow itself seems to have descended into hair, faces, shirts, and pants. These boys stood still just long enough to get their picture taken for the next page.

Read Before Starting Your Quilt on page 15.

Finished size: 56¾″ × 77″ (144.1 cm × 195.6 cm)
Finished size of blocks and alternate right blocks: 6″ × 8½″ (15.2 cm × 21.6 cm)
Finished size of alternate left blocks: 6¾″ × 8½″ (17.1 cm × 21.6 cm)
Number of blocks: 42
Blocks set: 7 × 6

YARDAGE

When assorted patterns and colors are used, allow slightly more fabric as the cutting is less efficient.

Background, sashing, first borders (blue): 3 yards (274 cm)
Figures (assorted colors)
    Hair: ½ yard (46 cm)
    Shirts: ½ yard (46 cm)
    Faces and hands: ¼ yard (23 cm)
    Socks, pants, shoes: Small amounts of many patterns and colors

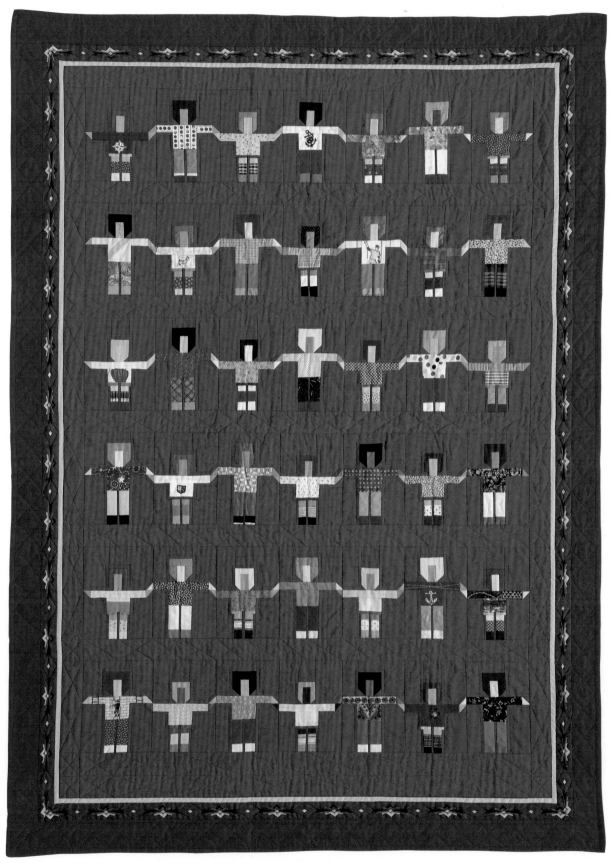

Designed by Jean Ray Laury, assembled and quilted by Bea Slater

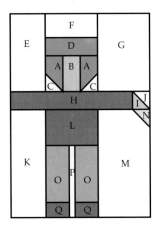

Big Brother
Make 15

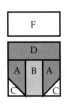

Step 1

Step 2

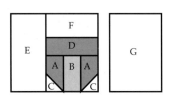

Step 3

Step 4

Second border (yellow, cut crosswise): ¼ yard (23 cm)

Third border (blue print, cut crosswise): ½ yard (46 cm)

Note: If you use a patterned fabric, as we did, allow extra to match print.

Fourth border and binding (red, cut crosswise): 1½ yards (137 cm)

Note: If you prefer borders and bindings on lengthwise grain, purchase the length of strips needed plus several inches' allowance.

Backing: 3½ yards (320 cm)

Batting: 61″ × 81″ (154.9 cm × 205.7 cm)

CUTTING

The diagrams show how the blocks are assembled and identify the pattern pieces. Templates are given for all pieces in the back of the book. Read all directions before beginning. An excess of 2″ (5.1 cm) is allowed on all long sashing and border strips, to be trimmed after sewing.

21 Big brother blocks

A	42 (flip for 21)
B, D, F, G, H, L, P	21 each
C, O, Q	42 each
E, K, M, N	18 each
I, J	24 each
Ea, Ka, Ma	3 each

21 Little brother blocks

A	42 (flip for 21)
B, D, F, H, L, M, R	21 each
C, O, P, Q, S, T	42 each
E, G, J, K	18 each
I, N	24 each
Ea, Ga, Ka	3 each

Sashing and first border (blue)

　　Sashing border: 5—2½″ × 45″ (6.4 cm × 114.3 cm)

　　Side border: 2—2½″ × 63″ (6.4 cm × 160 cm)

　　Top and bottom border: 3—2½″ × 49″ (6.4 cm × 124.5 cm)

Second border (yellow): 6—1″ (2.5 cm) strips × width of fabric

Third border (blue print): 8—2″ (5.1 cm) strips × width of fabric

Note: If you use a print or stripe for the border pattern, you will have to cut according to the design of your material. Be sure to add seam allowances.

Fourth border (red)

    Sides: 2—3″ × 80″ (7.6 cm × 203.2 cm)

    Top and bottom: 2—3″ × 60″ (7.6 cm × 152.4 cm)

    Note: Place on the lengthwise grain; cut borders before binding and smaller patterns.

Backing: 2—63″ (160 cm) lengths

Batting: 61″ × 81″ (154.9 cm × 205.7 cm)

Binding (red): 8—2½″ (6.4 cm) strips × width of fabric

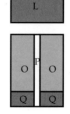

Step 5

CONSTRUCTING THE BLOCKS

Read all directions before starting. Keep a diagram or picture of the brother blocks on hand to guide you in assembling the parts.

If you use a single skin color for both sizes of brothers, you'll find the assembly greatly simplified. Just complete all the blocks as you go. If you use one skin color for big brother and a second color for little brother, you must be sure to use the appropriate colors where the hands touch. If you choose to work in a variety of skin colors, leave the hand seams open until you determine the final block placement. Then insert hand colors to match the adjoining faces.

Press all seams as you go. For example, after joining A, B, and A (step 2), press the seams before adding D.

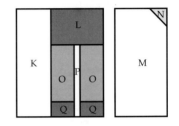

Step 6

BIG BROTHER BLOCKS

Make all big brother blocks first. The adjoining hand on the right side of each block will be in little brother's skin color.

1. Hair. Join C (background) to A (hair). Then join a flip of A to another C as shown in the diagram.

2. Head section. Join A to B (face) to flipped A. Add D (hair) then F (background).

3. Add backgrounds E and G to head.

4. Arm section. Join I (hand) in face color to J (background). Add this to the right end of H (arms) according to diagram.

5. Pants section. Join Os (legs) to Qs (feet), or use striped material to give a similar effect. Add to P (background), then to L (shirt).

6. Join N (hand of adjoining little brother) to M (background). Add pants section to backgrounds K and M.

7. Add arms section to head section. Add pants section to complete a big brother.

8. Now find the big brother for whom you are making this quilt and let him choose his own shirt print for the next block.

Repeat steps 1–7 to make a total of fifteen big brother blocks. Then make the alternate blocks as follows:

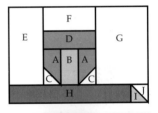

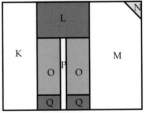

Step 7

BIG BROTHER ALTERNATE LEFT BLOCKS

Follow steps 1–7 for making a big brother block, substituting parts Ea and Ka for parts E and K. Add another J and I as shown in the diagram. You will now have a big brother with both a left and right hand as well as a connecting sibling's hand.

Repeat to make a total of three big brother alternate left blocks. You will use these blocks on the left edge of rows 2, 4, and 6.

BIG BROTHER ALTERNATE RIGHT BLOCKS

Follows steps 1–7 for making a big brother block, this time substituting part Ma for parts M and N. You will have a big brother with only one hand and no connecting sibling's hand.

Repeat to make a total of three big brother alternate right blocks. You will use these on the right edges of rows 2, 4, and 6.

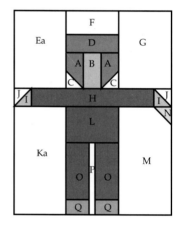 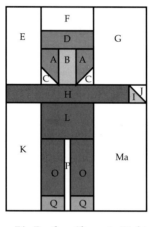

Big Brother Alternate Left
Make 3

Big Brother Alternate Right
Make 3

LITTLE BROTHER BLOCKS

Assembly for little brother is similar to that of big brother.

1. Hair. Join A (hair) to C (background). Then join a flip of A to another C as shown in the diagram.
2. Head section. Join A to B (face) to flipped A. Add D (hair) and F (background).
3. Join backgrounds E and G to head. Add J (hand of adjoining big brother) to G as shown in the diagram.
4. Arm section. Join I (hand—to match face color) to N (background). Add to end of H (arm).
5. Pants section. Join T (shoe) to S (sock) to Q (leg). Q should match face color. Add P (background) and then O (shorts)

according to diagram. Repeat for second leg. Next connect the legs with R (background); then add L (shirt). To simplify the piecing of the leg, use striped fabric to suggest shoes and socks, cutting them in one piece.

6. Join leg section to backgrounds K and M.

7. Join head section to arms, then add leg section to complete the block.

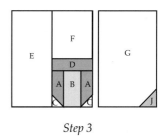

Step 3

Step 4

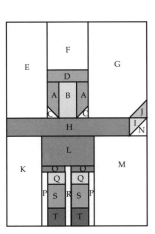

Little Brother
Make 15

Step 1

Step 2

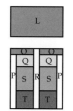

Step 5

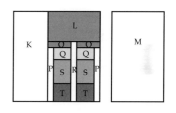

Step 6

Repeat steps 1–7 to make a total of fifteen little brother blocks. Then make the alternate blocks as follows:

LITTLE BROTHER ALTERNATE LEFT BLOCKS

Follow steps 1–7 for making a little brother, substituting parts Ea and Ka for parts E and K. Add another N and I as shown in the diagram. You will now have a little brother with both a left and right hand as well as a connecting sibling's hand.

Repeat to make a total of three little brother alternate left blocks. These will be used on the left edge of rows 1, 3, and 5.

LITTLE BROTHER ALTERNATE RIGHT BLOCKS

Follow steps 1–7 for making a little brother block, this time substituting part Ga for parts G and J. You will have a little brother with only one hand and no connecting sibling's hand.

Repeat to make a total of three little brother alternate right blocks. You will use these on the right edge of rows 1, 3, and 5.

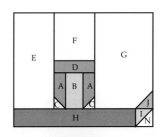

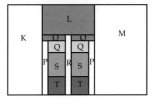

Step 7

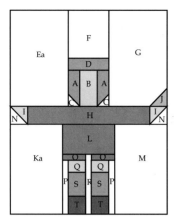

Little Brother Alternate Left
Make 3

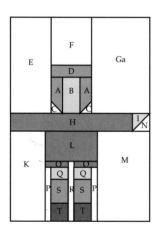

Little Brother Alternate Right
Make 3

ASSEMBLING THE QUILT TOP

1. Arrange the blocks to determine final placement. Use 7 figures in each row, and make 6 rows. Consult the diagram for proper placement of alternate blocks. If you have not already done so, insert the proper hand colors in each block and close those seams.

2. Join the big brothers and little brothers into rows.

3. Add the blue sashing strips between the rows of figures. This sashing is the same color as the block, which lets the figures float on the background.

ADDING BORDERS

1. Sew the first blue borders to the sides of the quilt top. Trim the ends flush with the blocks.

2. Add a blue border to the top and 2 blue border strips to the bottom, again trimming ends after sewing.

3. Join the ends of the yellow border strips with diagonal seams. Make 2 borders 50″ (127 cm) long and 2 borders 70″ (177.8 cm) long. Add the yellow borders to the quilt top, centering each border. Miter the corners.

4. Join the blue print strips to make 2 borders 54″ (137.2 cm) and 2 borders 74″ (188 cm) long. Piece with straight seams if you are using a repeat print. To center a repeat print in the border, fold fabric in half crosswise in the center of one of the repeat units. Match that spot to the center of the edge of your quilt. Repeat for bottom border, then add sides. Miter the corners.

5. Add the final wide red borders to the sides, then to top and bottom. Miter the corners. Trim and press.

Rows 1, 3, 5	Little Brother Alternate Left	Big Brother	Little Brother	Big Brother	Little Brother	Big Brother	Little Brother Alternate Right
Rows 2, 4, 6	Big Brother Alternate Left	Little Brother	Big Brother	Little Brother	Big Brother	Little Brother	Big Brother Alternate Right

Assembly Diagram

BACKING

1. The backing for this quilt is made by joining the selvage edges of two 63" (160 cm) lengths of fabric. Remove the selvages before sewing. The seamline will go across the back of the quilt and will allow 3" (7.6 cm) extra at each side. Trim top and bottom, leaving 2" to 3" (5.1 cm to 7.6 cm) excess at each end.

2. Open and spread the quilt batting in a large thin sheet. Stack backing, batting, and the quilt top for quilting, according to the general directions on page 117.

QUILTING

Our "human chain" of boys is machine quilted with a line that echoes the outline of the pieced figures. We used transparent nylon thread on the top, with sewing thread to match the backing fabric in the bobbin. All the seamlines of the sashing strips, borders, and blocks are quilted "in the ditch."

1. When quilting the five blue sashing strips between the rows of figures, continue these quilting lines through the first blue borders to the yellow borders. Do the same at the corners on the blue borders. These lines will later serve as a guide for the diamond quilting patterns. The layers are now secure and won't slip when the more intricate stitching is done.

2. Start the diamond quilting with the top blue border (the blue background color). It has one diamond corresponding to the space of one boy block. See A on the diagram (next page). The side points of the diamonds touch the seamlines just above the boys' heads at the top or between their feet at the bottom. Mark these points for your quilting guide. On the last block, next to the corner (B on the diagram), the diamond is compressed or squeezed to make an extra half diamond. That allows for a continuous line of quilting from the corner x into the border (see C on the diagram). There are 7 diamonds across, with 2 half diamonds at the ends. The same quilting pattern will be repeated on the bottom border.

3. At each side of the quilt, diamonds continue from the corner x's as they do in the top border. One side point of each diamond will touch a hand. Even though the hands are not precisely in the center of the blocks, it is visually better to have the quilting line touch the hands. See D in the quilting diagram. With this pattern, the border can be quilted in a continuous zigzag line that goes around all four sides. A second zigzag line of continuous quilting then crosses the first to complete the diamonds. *Note:* The yellow border has no quilting other than in-the-ditch stitching on each seamline.

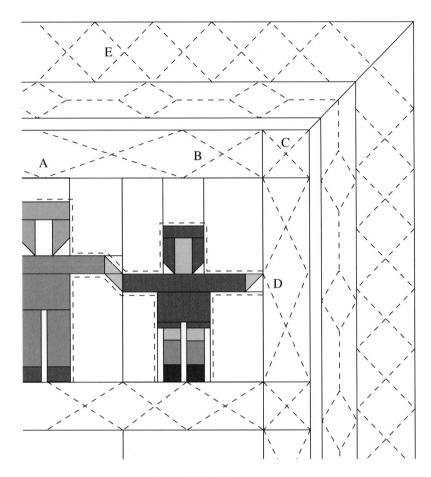

Brothers quilting diagram

4. The next border, in blue print, has been quilted with a pattern that picks up on the print design. You may wish to work out a pattern from the print you selected, or use a pattern of small diamonds connected by straight lines. Such quilting is accomplished with 2 steps. One continuous line forms half of each diamond and a line between the diamonds. The next line of quilting makes the second half of the diamond pattern.

5. The outer red border has rows of short, fat diamonds—almost checkerboard squares—stacked end to end. These are quilted in continuous lines as shown in E on the diagram. Quilts vary slightly in size because of cutting, seam widths, or quilting firmness, so you may have a measurement slightly different from ours. If your squares don't divide out evenly, you can start in the center at one side and let any discrepancies or changes be absorbed by the corner quilting pattern. Or you can start at the corners, and adjust the shapes at side centers to accommodate.

6. The final step is to outline each of the figures ¼″ (6 mm) away from the seamlines. Having secured the entire top with stitches, it will now be easier to maneuver the fabric and make the many turns.

BINDING

Join the binding strips with diagonal seams. Bind the quilt following the general directions on page 120. This quilt has a ½″ (13 mm) finished binding. Corners are mitered.

THE FINAL TOUCH

Now the gem who made this quilt should stitch her name into one of the diamonds of the blue border. Or better yet, fill a string of diamonds with important information about where and when. But don't let anyone *ever* forget the jewel who made this crew of colorful kids.

Designed by Jean Ray Laury, assembled and quilted by Jean Sayeg

Like some families, this mix-and-match series includes a brother/ sister combination. Ours has a big brother and a little sister, but they can be whisked off and replaced by big sister and little brother at the snip of your scissors.

Our *Big Brother/Little Sister* quilt has a definite thirties look, which comes from the limited palette of softened and grayed colors. It would be equally inviting in brights, in darks, or in variations of a single hue. A photograph of the quilt appears opposite.

Read Before Starting Your Quilt on page 15.

Finished size: 54¾" × 76½" (139.1 cm × 194.3 cm)
Finished size of blocks and alternate right blocks: 6" × 8½"
(15.2 cm × 21.6 cm)
Finished size of alternate left blocks: 6¾" × 8½"
(17.1 cm × 21.6 cm)
Number of blocks: 36
Blocks set: 6 × 6

YARDAGE

The design of this quilt lends itself especially well to the use of assorted scraps of prints and solids. Include a few plaids or patterns from outgrown clothes that the children can identify as their own. Remember that when you use a variety of fabrics, you will need slightly more fabric as the cutting is less efficient.

Background: 2 yards (183 cm)
Figures (assorted colors)
    Hair: ⅓ yard (31 cm)
    Face, hands, legs: ½ yard (46 cm)
    Clothes, shoes, socks: 1⅓ yards (122 cm)

Sashing (5 colors): each 2″ × 38″ (5.1 cm × 96.5 cm)
First border (teal): 1⅔ yards (152 cm)
Second border (lavender): 1¾ yards (160 cm)
Third border (deep lavender): 2 yards (183 cm)
Backing: 3⅓ yards (305 cm)
Batting: 59″ × 81″ (149.9 cm × 205.7 cm)
Binding: ⅔ yard (60 cm)

CUTTING

18 Big brothers

A	36 (flip for 18)
B, D, F, G, H, L, P	18 each
C, O, Q	36 each
E, K, M, N	15 each
I, J	21 each
Ea, Ka, Ma	3 each

18 Little sisters

A, O	36 each
B, C, D, G, K, L, M, P, Q	18 each
E, F, I, J, N	15 each
H	21
I	3 (in background color)
Ea, Fa, Ja, Na	3 each

Sashing strips (assorted fabrics): 5—2″ × 38″ (5.1 cm × 96.5 cm)
First border (teal)
    Sides: 2—2″ × 60″ (5.1 cm × 152.4 cm)
    Top and bottom: 2—2″ × 42″ (5.1 cm × 106.7 cm)
Second border (lavender)
    Sides: 2—3″ × 64″ (7.6 cm × 162.6 cm)
    Top and bottom: 2—3″ × 47″ (7.6 cm × 119.4 cm)
Third border (deep lavender)
    Sides: 2—5″ × 69″ (12.7 cm × 175.3 cm)
    Top and bottom: 2—5″ × 56″ (12.7 cm × 142.2 cm)
Backing: 2—59″ (149.9 cm) lengths
Batting: 59″ × 81″ (149.9 cm × 205.7 cm)
Binding (plaid): 8—2½″ (6.4 cm) strips × width of fabric

CONSTRUCTING THE BLOCKS

Along with the standard brother and sister blocks, you will make alternate left and right blocks for each, which will go on the outside edges of the rows. These blocks differ in the number and placement of

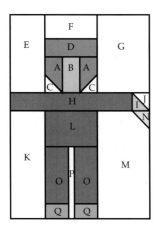

Big Brother
Make 12

hands—for example, an alternate right block will have no connecting sibling's hand because it will be placed at the right edge of a row.

If you use a single skin color for both the brother and sister blocks, you will find the assembly greatly simplified. Just complete the blocks as you go. If you select two skin colors, one for the boys and one for the girls, then you must use a big brother hand in the little sister block where the two join, and vice versa. Should you choose to work with a variety of skin colors, leave the hand seams open until you determine the final block placement. Hand colors can then be inserted to match the adjoining faces.

Press all seams as you go. For example, after joining A, B, and A, press seams carefully before you add the next piece. Any seam that will be crossed by another piece should be firmly pressed first.

BIG BROTHER BLOCKS

You will need to make a total of eighteen big brother blocks (twelve standard blocks, three big brother alternate left blocks, and three big brother alternate right blocks). See pages 31–32 for instructions.

The big brothers in this quilt all have cuffed pant legs. Create this cuffed look by piecing the leg or using a striped material.

LITTLE SISTER BLOCKS

You will need to make a total of eighteen little sister blocks (twelve standard blocks, three little sister alternate left blocks, and three little sister alternate right blocks). See pages 23–25 for instructions.

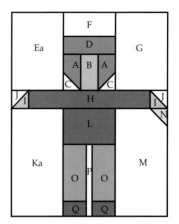

*Big Brother Alternate Left
Make 3*

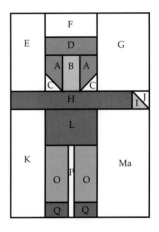

*Big Brother Alternate Right
Make 3*

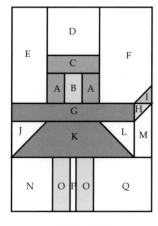

*Little Sister
Make 12*

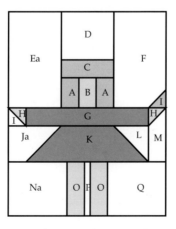

*Little Sister Alternate Left
Make 3*

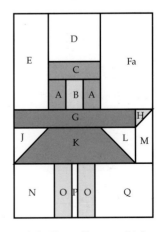

*Little Sister Alternate Right
Make 3*

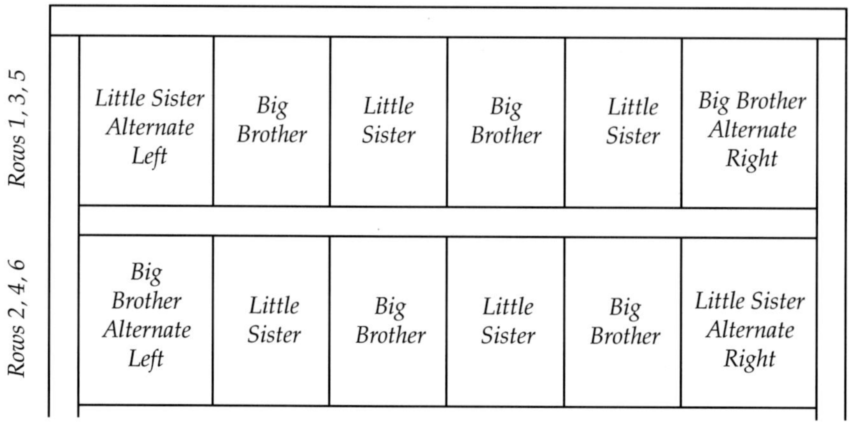
Rows 1, 3, 5
Little Sister Alternate Left
Big Brother
Little Sister
Big Brother
Little Sister
Big Brother Alternate Right
Rows 2, 4, 6
Big Brother Alternate Left
Little Sister
Big Brother
Little Sister
Big Brother
Little Sister Alternate Right

Assembly Diagram

ASSEMBLING THE QUILT TOP

1. Arrange the blocks, alternating brothers and sisters, to determine final placement. You will have 6 rows of 6 figures each. Use the diagram as a guide, noting where alternate blocks fall. If you have not already done so, insert the proper hand color in each block and close the seams.
2. Join the brothers and sisters in rows.
3. Now join the 6 rows of figures to the 5 sashing strips cut from assorted colors.

ADDING BORDERS

1. Pin the longer teal borders to the sides of the quilt. Sew and trim the ends. Then add the remaining teal borders to the top and the bottom. Trim.
2. Next pin the longer pale lavender borders to the sides; sew and trim. Add the remaining pale lavender borders to the top and bottom. Trim.
3. Finally, add the longer deep lavender borders to the sides and trim. Add the remaining borders to the top and bottom to complete the quilt top.

BACKING

1. Cut away the selvages and then join the backing pieces along the long sides. This seam will go across the width of the quilt. The seam can be centered, or it can be adjusted toward one end or the other, which will leave the excess fabric in one larger remnant instead of two smaller ones. Trim the backing to within 2″ to 3″

(5.1 cm to 7.6 cm) of the quilt top.

2. Lay out the backing with the batting to prepare for quilting, following our general directions on page 117.

QUILTING

This piece is hand quilted in threads that match the fabric colors.

1. First quilt lines within the horizontal sashing strips. These stitches are ¼" (6 mm) from the seamlines.

2. Next quilt the teal border, again with a ¼" (6 mm) space between the quilting and the seamline.

3. The pale lavender border is quilted in lines that parallel the long seamlines. The first row of stitching is ¼" (6 mm) from the seamline and the remaining rows are ½" (13 mm) apart.

4. In the dark lavender border, first quilt a line ¼" (6 mm) from the seamline. Then sew short quilting lines, ½" (13 mm) apart, across the border in groups of three. The lines start at the corner, and a 3" (7.6 cm) space is left between each group of lines. Use the photo as a guide for placement.

5. Complete the quilting by adding a line around each figure.

6. Trim edges.

BINDING

Madras plaid creates a multicolored and many-patterned binding that picks up most of the skirt and shirt hues. The binding finishes at ½" (13 mm) and goes on in one continuous strip. Refer to page 120 for complete instructions on applying the binding.

THE FINAL TOUCH

There is ample space for you to quilt your name right into the dark outer border. Add the date and place. And if you've already selected the lucky recipient for this work, include that name, too.

PIECED PUZZLE QUILTS

Jigsaw puzzles have an inexplicable appeal for most of us. Hours of a rainy weekend can slip by as we seek clues in curiously shaped pieces, trying to fit together parts that seem to have come from some other puzzle. Any individual piece offers few clues about the whole picture. Only when we assemble all the small parts do we see the entire image. The pieces in puzzle quilts are much the same. Individual shapes tell us nothing of the design, but once we piece the shapes together, we solve the puzzle, and a picture emerges.

In pieced puzzle quilts, the dark and light contrast between parts creates the image. A strong contrast makes an image very clear, as with our yellow geese on their dark backgrounds. Less contrast makes a more diffused or subtle picture. With no contrast at all, images will merge with the background, and all impact disappears.

It's fun to watch complex images or pictures emerge from the assembling of simple geometric shapes. This illusive quality in the design makes pieced puzzle quilts especially satisfying. They can be as obvious or as subtle as we choose. The ones shown here are brightly colored, and the images are clear, which makes them especially appealing to children, as well as fun to create.

In all pieced puzzle quilts, accurate seams are crucial to a perfect fit of the parts. The more seams there are, the more important this accuracy becomes. Be sure to adjust the width of your seams to conform with the seam allowance given on the patterns. You may find it helpful to use a small piece of tape on the feed-dog plate as a guide in maintaining consistent seam width.

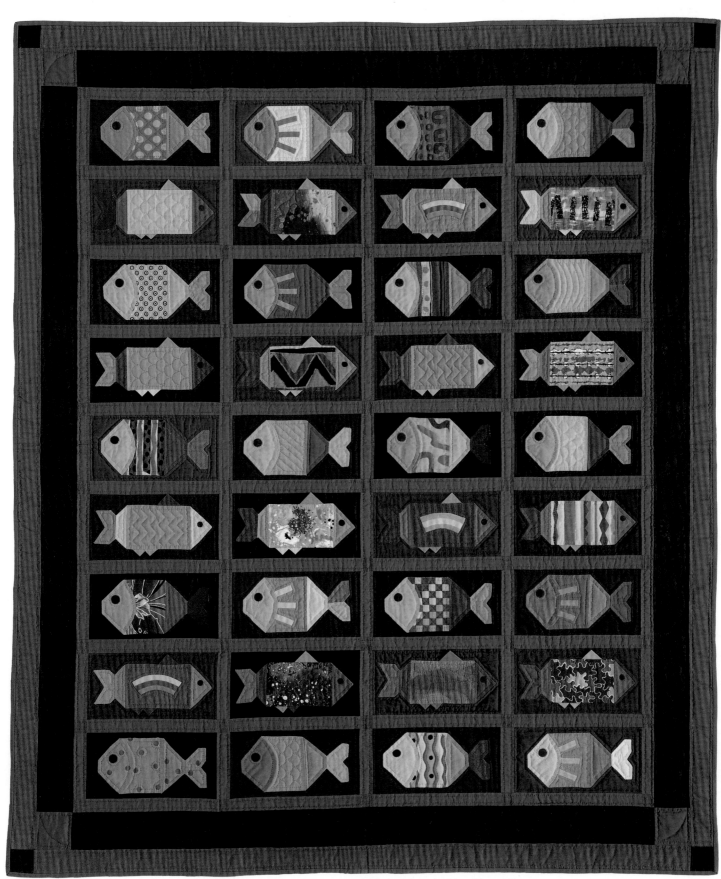

Designed by Jean Ray Laury, assembled and quilted by Cheryl Berman

FISH

Our quilt blocks stack up like aquarium tanks to display an entire school of tropical fish. Half of the fish appear to be migrating upstream while the rest float downstream. Some even appear luminous against the rich, dark backgrounds of their tanks.

Just two designs, and a constant juggling of colors and patterns, create a sea of riotous color. Salvage some of those wild shirts and surfer shorts that brighten kids' closets. You'll find yourself ready to snip a sleeve off a stranger's shirt because your sunfish *needs* that color. Or the temptation to clip a perfect scale pattern from your mother-in-law's dress may seem overpowering. But restrain yourself! You can combine bits and pieces of colors and scraps to get almost any effect you want. Bias tape offers a quick, effective way of adding lines. That's how we created the arcs on our rainbow trout and the rays on the sunfish.

A full-color picture of all three dozen fish appears on page 45. Read Before Starting Your Quilt on page 15.

Finished size: 66¾″ × 79″ (169.5 cm × 200.7 cm)
Finished size of blocks: 6″ × 12″ (15.2 cm × 30.5 cm)
Number of blocks: 36 (20 of Fish 1; 16 of Fish 2)
Blocks set: 4 × 9

YARDAGE

Background (blue): 2⅔ yards (243 cm), if you use a single color
Note: In assorted colors, ½ yard (46 cm) will provide 6 blocks. This quilt uses 7 different colors for the blocks.
Fish: 2⅔ yards (243 cm), if you use one color
Note: Each fish requires about a 6″ × 14″ (15.2 cm × 35.6 cm) piece of fabric, but if you use many different patterns, you will need more fabric. Start with scraps and remnants you have, and go from there.

Ultra Suede® (or any similar nonwoven, suedelike material) 6″ × 6″ (15.2 cm × 15.2 cm) scraps in assorted colors for eyes (optional)

Sashing strips, border squares, binding (blue-green): 2 yards (183 cm)

First border (navy): 2 yards (183 cm)

Second border and sashing squares (violet): 2¼ yards (206 cm)

Interfacing: 4 yards (366 cm), 18″ (45.7 cm) wide

Note: Use a thin, lightweight, nonwoven, nonfusible material. Each fish is faced.

Backing: 4 yards (366 cm)

Batting: 70″ × 82″ (177.8 cm × 208.3 cm)

CUTTING

Fish 1

A, B, C, E	20 each
D	40 (flip for 20)

Fish 2

F	32 (flip for 16)
G, H, I, J, K	16 each
L	32

Note: If you use Ultra Suede® for the eyes, do not add seam allowance. If you use a polka-dot fabric, add the seam allowance shown on the template.

Background blocks (dark colors): 36—6½″ × 12½″ (16.5 cm × 31.8 cm)

Interfacing rectangles: 36—6″ × 12″ (15.2 cm × 30.5 cm)

Sashing strips, border squares, binding (blue-green)

    Side sashing: 45—1¾″ × 6½″ (4.4 cm × 16.5 cm)

    Top and bottom sashing: 40—1¾″ × 12½″ (4.4 cm × 31.8 cm)

    Squares: 4—4″ × 4″ (10.2 cm × 10.2 cm)

    Binding: 8—2½″ (6.4 cm) strips × width of fabric

First borders and border squares (navy)

    Sides: 2—4″ × 69″ (10.2 cm × 175.3 cm)

    Top and bottom: 2—4″ × 56¾″ (10.2 cm × 144.1 cm)

    Squares: 4—2¾″ × 2¾″ (7 cm × 7 cm)

Second borders and sashing squares (violet)

    Side borders: 2—2¾″ × 76″ (7 cm × 193 cm)

    Top and bottom borders: 2—2¾″ × 63¾″ (7 cm × 161.9 cm)

    Squares: 50—1¾″ × 1¾″ (4.4 cm × 4.4 cm)

Backing: 2—72″ (183 cm) lengths

Batting: 70″ × 82″ (177.8 cm × 208.3 cm)

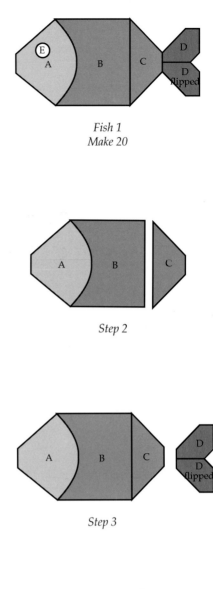

Fish 1
Make 20

Step 2

Step 3

Fish 2
Make 16

Step 4

CONSTRUCTING THE BLOCKS

1. Make up 20 of Fish 1 and 16 of Fish 2.

2. Fish 1. Join the curved seam of A to B; add C.

3. Join a D to a flipped D to form tail and add to C. Appliqué an eye (E) in place. Eyes cut from polka dot fabric, with one dot dead-center, give a wall-eyed effect. The very small circles for the eyes are sometimes difficult for beginning quilters to appliqué, and you may wish to substitute the optional nonwoven material. If your quilt is for a kid of 40, you may wish to use lamé fabrics, glass beads, or wiggly eyes.

4. Fish 2. Join an F to a flipped F to make tail. Add to G, H, and I. Appliqué an eye (J) in place.

5. Fins. Folded squares, or "prairie points," make fins for Fish 2. Fold a K square in half diagonally. Then fold it again to make a right-angle triangle with the four open edges together. Press. Stitch across the open end ⅛" (3 mm) from the raw edge. Make 16 fins from the K squares and 32 fins from the L squares.

6. Place a large prairie point fin (K) at the top edge (right sides facing) of an assembled Fish 2, aligning the raw edges of the fin with the raw edge of the fish. Use the diagram as a guide. Fin should be 1" (2.5 cm) in back of the head/body seam.

7. Place 2 small prairie point fins (L) side by side on the bottom edge of the fish, 3" (7.6 cm) in back of the head/body seam. Pin or baste to keep the fins from moving.

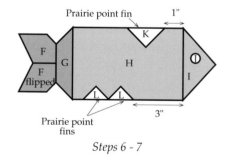

Steps 6 - 7

8. Cut a piece of interfacing about 1" (2.5 cm) bigger on all edges than a fish. Place the assembled fish, which has been carefully pressed, face down on the interfacing. Pin or baste. When working with a Fish 2, be sure the prairie point fins are inserted correctly.

9. Stitch around the outside edge of the fish on the seam line. Trim corners and clip as necessary.

10. Cut a slit in the interfacing at center back. Turn the fish right side out.

11. Smooth the edges and press. You will have a finished edge on the fish body. If you are working with a Fish 2, the prairie point fins will extend from the fish's body. The white interfacing should not show on the front surface. If yours peeks out, roll the edge of the fish just slightly over the interfacing and tack or baste in place until the piece is appliquéd to a background. Interfacing also comes in black, which may show up less on a dark background.

12. Your fish can be made more exotic through various embellishments. Some of ours have appliquéd shapes, though most are "plain" and depend upon the fabric prints for the decorative designs.

13. Fold the background fabrics in half, lengthwise. Place each fish onto a background and align the points of nose and tail with the fold line. Appliqué the fish body in place by hand, using a matching thread and a blind stitch. The prairie point fins remain free to stand out slightly from the quilt. Because the edges of the fish are pre-finished, the appliqué is simple and speedy.

ASSEMBLING THE QUILT TOP

1. When all the fish blocks are appliquéd, lay them out on the floor, or any large area, and arrange them, referring to the photo for placement. You may prefer mixing the 2 designs to placing all of one design in a row.

2. Sew a short sashing to the left side of each fish and join the blocks in rows of 4. You will have 9 rows.

3. Add another short sashing to the far right edge in each row.

4. Join 4 long sashings to 5 violet squares, beginning with a square and alternating to form a strip. You will need 10.

5. Add a long pieced sashing strip to the top of each row of fish, matching all seamlines.

6. Sew the rows together. Add the last pieced sashing strip to the bottom edge.

ADDING BORDERS

1. Add the long navy borders to the sides of the quilt. Trim ends even with the sashing strips.

2. Then join one of the blue-green squares to one end of the top navy border. Sew to the top edge of the quilt, starting with the square, to within 8″ (20.3 cm) of the second corner. Measure the remaining border to the end, allowing for ¼″ (6 mm) seam, trim, and add a second square. Sew the rest of the border to the quilt top. Repeat for the bottom border.

3. Add the long violet borders to the sides of the quilt.

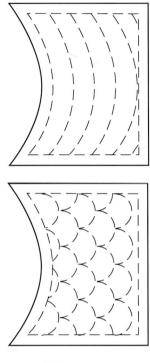

Quilting patterns
Fish 1

Quilting patterns
Fish 2

4. Join navy squares to one end of the top and bottom violet borders, and follow the instructions in step 2 to finish the quilt top.

BACKING

1. Once the 4 yard (366 cm) length of backing fabric has been cut into 2 lengths of 2 yards (183 cm) each, trim the selvages and join the fabrics on the long sides. Press. This will make one horizontal seam on the back of the finished quilt. Do not trim the backing until it has been stacked with the batting and quilt top.
2. Layer the backing, seam side up, with batting and quilt top according to the complete directions given on page 117.

QUILTING

Our quilt is hand quilted in colors that vary according to the color upon which they are sewn. The overall quilting pattern consists of lines that parallel the seamlines. The lines run ¼" (6 mm) from the edges, including inside and outside the appliqué. The wide blue border is quilted with a swag pattern. Each swag, or half circle, touches the edge of a violet sashing square, and a second line of stitches repeats the same ¼" (6 mm) parallel line of the block quilting. Consult the photograph for details.

Each of the fish parts is highlighted by an outline of quilting. The quilting patterns on the fish vary, as most are quilted according to the fabric print. Some plain fish have scales quilted in a miniature scallop while others wear stripes or diamonds. See the quilting patterns for ideas. Printed fabrics have quilting that meanders along printed lines of stripes or flowers.

BINDING

Join the binding strips with diagonal seams. Follow our directions for adding binding on page 120. The binding on this quilt finishes at ½" (13 mm) wide.

THE FINAL TOUCH

Now appliqué "the one that got away" on the reverse side of the quilt, and use that fish for your signature and pertinent information.

Your admirers will not be limited to kids. Grown men are going to be angling for this well-stocked pool of fish. They'll go "hook, line, and sinker" for your creation, so it might be a good idea to identify the owner of this catch as well.

CREEPY CRAWLIES

Our *Creepy Crawlies* will win the hearts of all kids who carry toads in their pockets or collect tadpoles in mayonnaise jars. "Snips and snails and puppy-dog tails . . . that's what little boys are made of." And you can bet they'll love having these colorful serpents slithering all over their bedcovers.

I have known a few girls to be avid snake collectors, too, so we should avoid any quick assumptions about who will become our future herpetologists. These snakes are, of course, huggable and harmless, or we wouldn't invite them into our workbaskets. In the "real world," their mere appearance in such resplendent patterns would endanger their very existence; every collector would relish one. The best way for *us* to collect them is on fabric, so we can stitch them firmly into our quilts.

Once you start assembling these vivid reptiles, you will see fabric in a whole new way. "Aha, snake skin!" you'll shout in the quilt shop when you spot a diamond pattern. The tricolored bands of a king snake, or the brilliant green stripes of a garter snake will entice you from their bolts. The perfect pattern for a boa constrictor may appear in the blouse of a quilting friend, as printed designs take on new meanings. The fun of making this quilt compensates for the raised eyebrows of quilting friends or skeptical relatives. The kids on your block will eagerly check your studio for the newest captives, with bright ideas for naming any unidentified specimens.

Several full-grown adults I know have already hinted broadly for a quilt chock-full of these creepy crawlies. My own preference is for the nonvenomous looking serpents in polka dots, ginghams, and large florals.

The entire collection of snakes appears in the photograph on the next page.

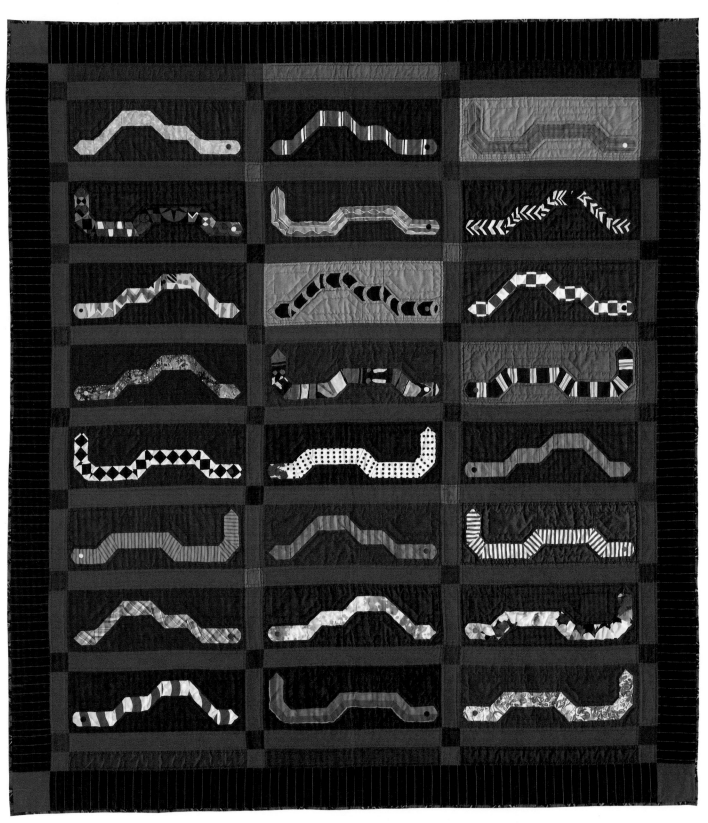

Designed by Jean Ray Laury, assembled and quilted by Nancy Clemmensen

Read Before Starting Your Quilt on page 15.

Finished size: 74″ × 83″ (188 cm × 210.8 cm)
Finished size of blocks: 6½″ × 19″ (16.5 cm × 48.3 cm)
Number of blocks: 24 (12 of Snake 1; 12 of Snake 2)
Note: Some of the snakes may be reversed in direction or placed upside down to give greater variety to the overall pattern.
Blocks set: 3 × 8

YARDAGE

Background (assorted colors): 2 yards (183 cm) total
Note: ½ yard (45.8 cm) is ample for 4 background blocks. If you use a variety of colors, you will need to allow additional fabric as the cutting is less efficient.
Snakes: 2 yards (183 cm)
Note: ⅓ yard (31 cm) is ample for 4 snakes, but you will need additional fabric to match stripes or plaids.
Sashing and squares (red): 1¾ yards (160 cm)
Sashing and squares (assorted colors): ⅔ yard (60 cm)
Or you may wish to use fabric left over from the cutting of background pieces.
Borders (striped): 1¼ yards (114 cm)
Backing: 4⅓ yards (397 cm)
Batting: 78″ × 87″ (198.1 cm × 221 cm)
Binding (print): ¾ yard (69 cm)

CUTTING

Background

Snake 1 A–K	12 each
Snake 2 L–V	12 each

Snake parts

Snake 1 1–7	12 each
Snake 2 8–14	12 each

Note: If you wish to reverse the direction of a snake, you must flip all of the pattern parts (both snake and background) for that block if you are using a print. Many solid colors are reversible, so they could be flipped before sewing.

Sashing and squares (red)

Long sashing: 27—2½″ × 19½″ (6.4 × 49.5 cm)
Short sashing: 32—2½″ × 7″ (6.4 cm × 17.8 cm)
Small squares: 8—2½″ × 2½″ (6.4 cm × 6.4 cm)
Large squares: 4—4½″ × 4½″ (11.4 cm × 11.4 cm)

Sashing and squares (assorted colors)

    Sashing: 6—2½″ × 19½″ (6.4 cm × 49.5 cm)

    Squares: 36—2½″ × 2½″ (6.4 cm × 6.4 cm)

Borders

    Sides: 2—4½″ × 76″ (11.4 cm × 193 cm)

    Top and bottom: 2—4½″ × 67″ (11.4 cm × 170.2 cm)

Note: Fabric stripes usually run lengthwise, so for crosswise stripes, border pieces must be cut across the grain. Straight seams will be preferable to diagonal as it is difficult to match stripes on the diagonal. A straight seam will disappear into the stripes.

Backing: 2—78″ (198.1 cm) lengths

Batting: 78″ × 87″ (198.1 cm × 221 cm)

Binding: 8—2½″ (6.4 cm) strips × width of fabric

CONSTRUCTING THE BLOCKS

The templates are identified with letters for the background pieces and numbers for the snake parts. The snake part templates are shaded. You may find other sequences for joining the blocks, depending upon how easily you manage corner seams. When sewing into a corner, stop stitching ¼″ (6 mm) away from the end of the seam to make turning the corner easier. *Note:* Do not sew into the seam allowance.

You will find it helpful to do a mock-up of the block in paper. Then place your pattern parts on top of it for a quick reference as you sew. Place all the cut pieces for one snake in order before you begin sewing. Refer to the diagrams as you work.

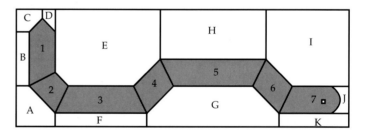

Snake 1
Make 12

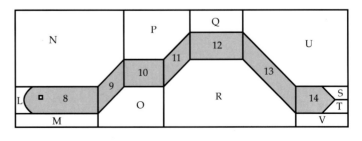

Snake 2
Make 12

SNAKE 1

1. To make unit 1, join backgrounds B and C, add to snake part 1. Then add D. Join A to snake part 2 and add to first section.

2. To make unit 2, join F to snake part 3 and add to E.

3. To make unit 3, join H to snake part 5, and join G to snake part 4. Join sections to form unit 3.

4. To make unit 4, join background J to snake part 7, then add K and snake part 6. Add background piece I.

5. Join units 1, 2, 3, and 4.

6. Repeat steps 1–5 until you have 12 of Snake 1. If you flipped the pattern parts to reverse a snake, follow the same steps, but the sewing will begin at the right side instead of the left.

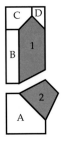

Unit 1
Step 1

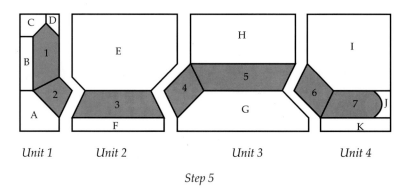

Unit 1   Unit 2   Unit 3   Unit 4

Step 5

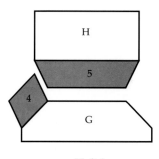

Unit 2
Step 2

SNAKE 2

7. To make unit 5, join background L to snake part 8. Add backgrounds M and N.

8. To make unit 6, join snake parts 9, 10, and 11. Add O then join to P.

9. To make unit 7, join snake part 12 to Q and then add R.

10. To make unit 8, join snake part 14 to S and T. Add snake part 13 and U, then add V.

11. Join units 5, 6, 7, and 8 to complete the block.

12. Repeat steps 7–11 until you have 12 of Snake 2. If you flipped the pattern parts to reverse a snake, follow the same steps, but the sewing will begin at the right side instead of the left.

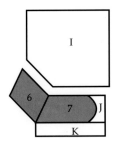

Unit 3
Step 3

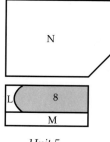

Unit 5
Step 7

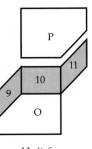

Unit 6
Step 8

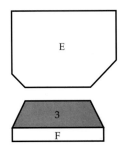

Unit 4
Step 4

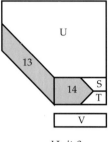

Unit 7
Step 9

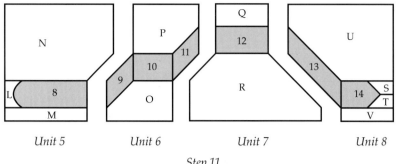

Unit 5　　*Unit 6*　　*Unit 7*　　*Unit 8*

Step 11

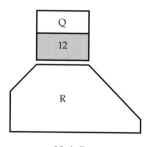

Unit 8
Step 10

Add eyes to complete the snakes. The eyes on our snakes were appliquéd from a nonwoven, suedelike cloth, so it was not necessary to add a seam allowance. Check your material for colorfastness by washing a small piece and ironing it dry.

ASSEMBLING THE QUILT TOP

Now using the photograph for reference, lay out your blocks.

1. To assemble the *Creepy Crawlies* quilt top, add a short red sashing strip to the left side of each block.
2. Then assemble a row of 3 blocks across, adding another short sashing strip at the right-hand edge. You will need to have 8 rows assembled in this way.
3. Sew 4 small assorted colored squares to 3 long red sashing strips, starting with a square and alternating to form a row. Repeat to form 9 rows.
4. Sew a row of sashing to the bottom of each row of snake blocks, carefully aligning so that all seams meet. Repeat for all rows. Sew all rows together. Add a final row of sashing to the top edge.
5. Additional rows of sashing are used at the top and bottom of the quilt in colors that alternate with the sashing already in place. Join small red squares to the colored sashing strips and add to top and bottom edges, aligning seams.

ADDING BORDERS

1. Add one of the longer striped borders to each side of the quilt top. Trim so that ends are even.
2. Add one large red square to one end of each of the remaining borders. Pin a border to the top of the quilt, aligning red square to side striped border. Sew to within about 8″ (20.3 cm) of the end. Measure, trim, and add the second square to the end of the border. Sew to quilt top. Repeat for the bottom of the quilt.

BACKING

1. Join the two 78" (198.1 cm) lengths, removing selvages before sewing. This will give you one horizontal seam across the quilt back. Do not trim, as you will need the excess fabric during quilting.

2. Stack the backing, batting, and quilt top according to our directions on page 117.

QUILTING

Our snakes are hand quilted with a deep red thread. Refer to complete directions on page 118. Quilting lines run parallel to the seamlines of all sashes and borders, ¼" (6 mm) from each seam. Each snake is quilted ¼" (6 mm) from the seamline. Inside each block, a second line of quilting is added ½" (13 mm) beyond the first. See the photo on page 52 for reference.

BINDING

Creepy Crawlies is now ready for binding. We used a printed fabric cut on the crosswise grain and pieced with diagonal seams. The binding finishes ½" (13 mm) wide. The corners are squared. See page 120 for complete directions on binding.

THE FINAL TOUCH

Now, for heaven's sake, get these ridiculous reptiles out of your lap. Write a label that clearly identifies the new zookeeper responsible for their care. Be sure to date their appearance on the scene, and sign yourself as the collector and trainer.

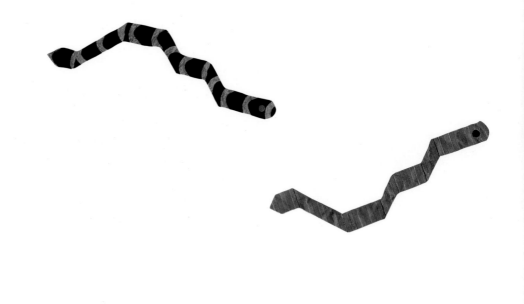

GOOSIE GOOSIE GANDER

Geese appear with inexplicable frequency in children's stories. My own experience with geese is that they nip unmercifully at your heels when you walk anywhere near them. But, from "The Goose Girl" to Mother Goose, they waddle through children's fiction in flocks or paddle forward single file. Their presence in stories has endeared them to children for centuries.

Here an entire gaggle of geese comes waddling along. Assorted bright, clear yellows make up the geese and their wings, while random combinations of vivid oranges and reds are used for the beaks and feet.

The geese are lined up for a group photo on the next page. Read Before Starting Your Quilt on page 15.

Finished size: 61″ × 73″ (154.9 cm × 185.4 cm)
Finished size of blocks: 12″ × 15″ (30.5 cm × 38.1 cm)
Number of blocks: 16
Blocks set: 4 × 4

YARDAGE

Fabric requirements are based on single pieces of yardage. If you use scraps, there will be more waste, so you will need to allow additional fabric.

Background, second border (printed fabric): 4½ yards (411 cm)
Note: If you select a print that must be matched when the border is pieced, you will need to allow an extra ⅓ yard (31 cm) of fabric.
Bodies of geese (yellows, assorted): 1⅔ yards (152 cm)
Beaks, feet, small squares in first border (oranges, assorted): ½ yard (46 cm)
First border (deep orange): ⅔ yard (60 cm)
Backing: 3¾ yards (343 cm)

Designed by Jean Ray Laury, assembled and quilted by Bea Slater

Batting: 64″×76″ (162.6 cm×193 cm)

Binding (yellow print): ⅔ yard (60 cm)

CUTTING

Each goose block

    Yellow

3	4
7, 10, 11, 14, 16, 18, 19	1 each

    Dark yellow (wings)

10, 17	1 each

    Orange (beaks, feet)

3	6
7, 21	2 each
10	1

    Background print

3	5
4	3
10, 20	2 each
1, 2, 5, 6, 8, 9,	1 each
12, 13, 15, 22–27	

First border (dark orange)

    Top and bottom: 6—15¼″×2½″ (38.7 cm×6.4 cm)

    Sides: 8—14″×2½″ (35.6 cm×6.4 cm)

Border squares (orange): 14—2½″×2½″ (6.4 cm×6.4 cm)

Second border (backgound print, cut crosswise): 6—4½″ (11.4 cm) strips×width of fabric

Note: You will need 1 or 2 additional strips if you match prints; piece as necessary.

Backing: 2—64″ (162.6 cm) lengths

Batting: 64″×76″ (162.6 cm×193 cm)

Binding: 8—2½″ (6.4 cm) strips×width of fabric

CONSTRUCTING THE BLOCKS

The *Goosie Goosie Gander* block is divided into sections to simplify the assembly, as shown in the diagrams. Sections are given letters, while each pattern part is identified by number.

Assembling pieces in order before you begin to sew will speed the process. You may find it helpful to place the cut pieces on half sheets of paper with identifying numbers written clearly on the paper. Then when you need a blue 3 you can quickly identify it and pick it up. Press all seams as you go. Assemble as follows:

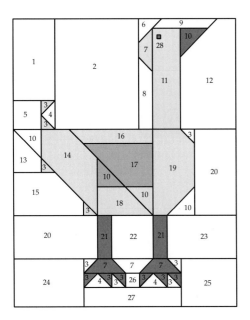

Goosie Goosie Gander
Make 16

1. To make section A, sew two yellow 3s (small triangles) to blue 4 (triangle), then to blue 5 and to blue 1.

2. To make section B, add yellow 7 to blue 8 and then join to yellow 11. Add orange 10 to blue 12, leaving 1" (2.5 cm) of the top end of the seam open to make later joins easier, then join to 11. Add 9 at the top and close the seamline at orange 10. Complete by sewing 6 onto the corner. Add blue 2 to the left side. Join section A to B.

3. To make section C, join blue 13 to yellow 3, add to blue 15, then add second yellow 3.

4. To make section D, join dark yellow 10 (wing) to yellow 18 (body), then add yellow 14 and blue 10.

5. To make section E, join yellow 10 to dark yellow 17 (wing) and add yellow 16.

6. To make section F, add blue 10 to yellow 19 and blue 3. Add blue 20. Join sections C, D, E, and F.

7. To make section G, start with blue 20; join to orange 21, to blue 22, to orange 21, and to blue 23.

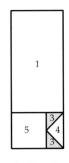

Section A

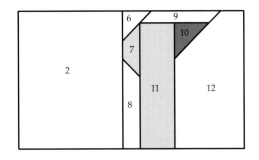

Section B

Section E

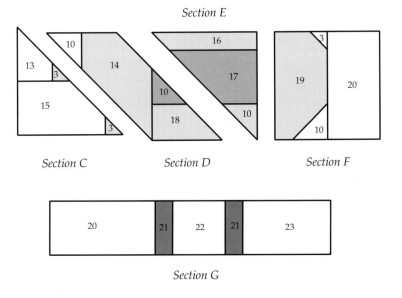

| *Section C* | *Section D* | *Section F* |

Section G

8. To make section H (tops of feet) join blue 3 to orange 7 to blue 7 to orange 7 to blue 3. (See diagram on next page.)

9. To make section I (toes), from left to right, join orange 3 to blue 4 to orange 3. Then add blue 3 and orange 3. Repeat for second foot. Then join the feet by adding blue 26 between them.

10. Join sections H, I, and J (27).

11. Add sections K (24) and L (25).

12. Press sections again, then join as shown to form a block, and watch your goose emerge from all the bits and pieces.

13. Repeat steps 1–12 until you have 16 geese.

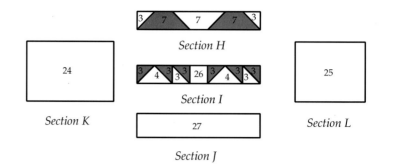

Section H

Section I

Section K   *Section L*

Section J

14. Should you choose to add eyes, appliqué them before you assemble the quilt top. Use one of the fabrics that already appears in your quilt, or use any contrasting color. Substituting a suedelike, nonwoven cloth will ease the appliqué of these tiny circles as edges do not need to be turned under. If you choose a nonwoven fabric, do not add the seam allowance shown on the template. Our black-eyed geese have suede-cloth eyes.

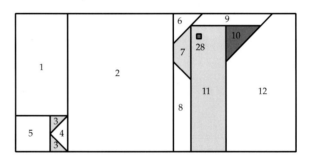

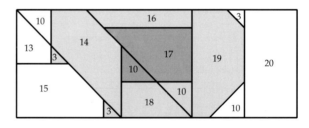

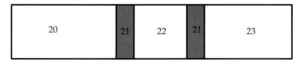

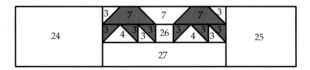

Step 12

ASSEMBLING THE QUILT TOP

1. Arrange the 16 blocks in 4 rows of 4 geese each.
2. Join the blocks to make 4 rows.
3. Join the rows together, matching seams.
4. Press the quilt top.

ADDING BORDERS

1. For the first top border, join 3 of the longer dark orange strips to 2 of the orange squares, starting with a strip and alternating. Sew to the top of the quilt. Repeat for bottom edge. Trim.
2. For each of the first side borders of the quilt, alternate 4 of the shorter dark orange strips with 5 of the orange squares, beginning and ending with a square. Add one strip to each side. The orange squares should fit exactly in the corners.
3. The second border, cut from the background print, is added next. Join the 4½" (11.4 cm) strips end to end. Cut two borders 54½" (138.4 cm) long. Place a border on the top of the quilt, and join it to the first border. Repeat for bottom. Trim ends.
4. Cut two borders 74½" (189.2 cm) long. Place one border at the side of the quilt and join. Add remaining border to the other side. Trim ends.

BACKING

1. Remove selvages and join the 2 lengths of fabric on the long sides. Trim to 64" × 76" (162.6 cm × 193 cm). This will make one horizontal seam across the back of the quilt.
2. Place the backing, batting, and quilt top together according to the directions on page 117. The backing and batting will be a few inches larger than the quilt top and should be left until quilting is completed.

QUILTING

Goosie Goosie Gander is machine quilted using a free-form design that follows the floral print of the background fabric. A cotton thread was used in the bobbin with a dark nylon thread on the top for the dark fabrics. For light fabrics (yellows and oranges), light nylon was used.

1. Quilt "in the ditch" on both seamlines of the orange border. That will secure all the layers of the quilt.
2. Quilt a series of x's within the orange border. Start by sewing half an x on a light orange square and continue zigzaging around the border. Repeat the zigzag, crossing over the first lines to

complete the x's. In the dark orange areas, each x needs to be stretched just slightly. By "fudging" about ⅛" (3 mm) on each x, you will have 6 x's on each dark orange border. This allows you to quilt the entire border in a continuous line.

3. Outline each goose with quilting "in the ditch." Additional lines are quilted within the goose.

4. Use free-form quilting over the print of your fabric to create an allover pattern of stitches in the background of the blocks and in the wide final border.

BINDING

We have used a yellow printed binding, which finishes at ½" (13 mm) wide. Piece the strips with diagonal seams. Add the squared binding according to the general directions on page 120.

THE FINAL TOUCH

Don't be a silly goose by failing to sign and date your quilt. It'll be a (goose) feather in your quilting cap. The name of the gosling for whom the quilt was made would be a nice addition.

THIS LITTLE PIGGY

"This little piggy went to market" is a rhyme familiar to almost every child. The toe-wiggling part, "This little piggy cried, 'wee, wee, wee' all the way home," brings shrill giggles from even the most sober youngster. Part of the giggling comes from being ticklish, but part of it stems from the fact that pigs are *messy*. And messiness strikes at the funny bone of most kids. Pigs get to slosh in the mud and have terrible manners. That alone would make them irresistible, even without their curly tails. Who wouldn't love a piglet? They're harmless, roly-poly, and abundantly popular in stories. The "Three Little Pigs" are as dear to children as *Winnie-the-Pooh*'s Piglet and *Charlotte's Web*'s Wilbur.

So here is a quilt for the consummate young pig fancier. White and black patterns recall the folk song in which "Sweet Betsy from Pike" comes West with her "one spotted hog." Whatever your child's favorite pig story, here's a way to bring pigs into the house without the pigsty.

Our piggies posed with their best sides to the camera for the next page. Can you find the one who changed his mind and turned around?

Read Before Starting Your Quilt on page 15.

Finished size: 58½" × 74½" (148.6 cm × 189.2 cm)
Finished size of blocks: 7½" × 11" (19.1 cm × 27.9 cm)
Number of blocks: 32 (16 coming and 16 going)
Blocks set: 4 × 8

YARDAGE

Note: Remember that when you use assorted colors, you will need additional yardage as the cutting is less efficient.
Background (assorted greens): 2⅔ yards (243 cm)
⅓ yard (31 cm) will be enough for 5 background blocks.

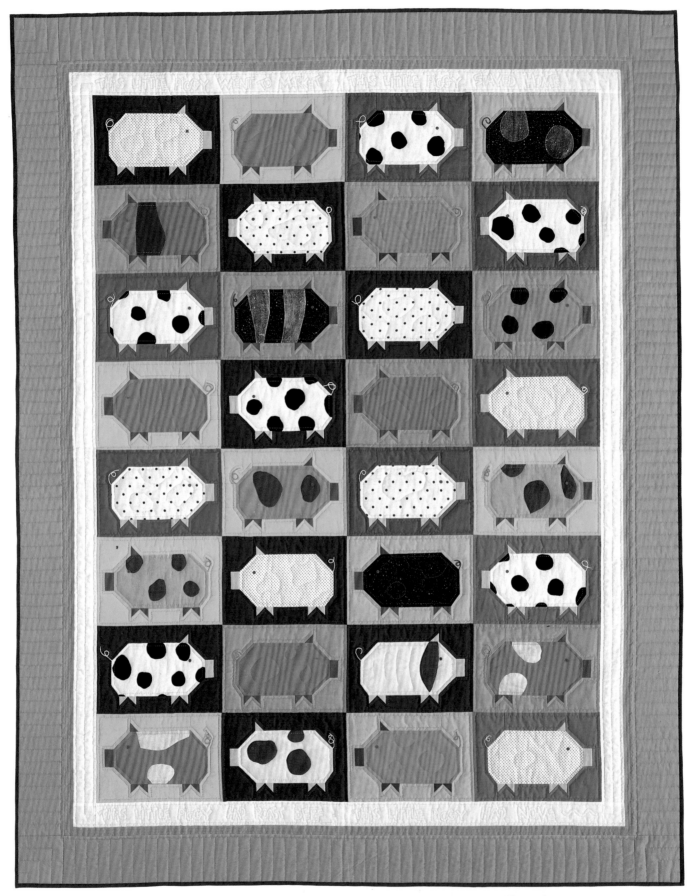

Designed by Jean Ray Laury, assembled and quilted by Marguerite Shattuck

Pigs (polka dots, spots, or solids): 1 yard (91 cm)
¼ yard (23 cm) will give you 8 pigs.
Noses, ears, feet (assorted pinks): ½ yard (46 cm)
Allow a 4″ × 6″ (10.2 cm × 15.2 cm) piece for each pig.
First border (white): 1¾ yards (160 cm)
Second border (pink): 2 yards (183 cm)
Third border (green): 2 yards (183 cm)
Note: If the pink and green used in the borders are also used in the blocks, purchase only the border yardage as there will be ample excess for other parts. Also, border yardage is based on lengthwise cuts so that no seams appear in the borders.
Backing: 3½ yards (320 cm)
Batting: 63″ × 79″ (160 cm × 200.6 cm)
Binding (dark green): ½ yard (46 cm)

CUTTING

If you wish half of your pigs to go to the right while half head to the left, as ours do, flip the pattern parts for sixteen of the blocks. Keep the pigs heading east separate from those heading west.

Background (assorted greens)

A, H	64 each
B, C, E, G, I, J	32 each

Pigs (black, white, pink, polka dot, or printed)

F	32

Note: Flowered prints will make wonderful "china pigs." Or you may wish to appliqué, stencil, or paint the spots on fabric if you cannot locate suitable polka dots.

Noses, ears, feet (assorted pinks)

D	160 (5 for each pig)
E	32

First border (white)
> **Sides:** 2—2½″ × 62½″ (6.4 cm × 158.8 cm)
> **Top and bottom:** 2—2½″ × 46½″ (6.4 cm × 118.1 cm)
> **Corner squares:** 4—2½″ × 2½″ (6.4 cm × 6.4 cm)

Second border (pink)
> **Sides:** 2—1¼″ × 66½″ (3.2 cm × 168.9 cm)
> **Top and bottom:** 2—1¼″ × 50½″ (3.2 cm × 128.3 cm)
> **Corner squares:** 4—1¼″ × 1¼″ (3.2 cm × 3.2 cm)

Third border (green)
> **Sides:** 2—4½″ × 68″ (11.4 cm × 172.7 cm)
> **Top and bottom:** 2—4½″ × 52″ (11.4 cm × 132.1 cm)
> **Corner squares:** 4—4½″ × 4½″ (11.4 cm × 11.4 cm)

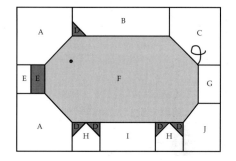

Piggy Block Coming
Make 16

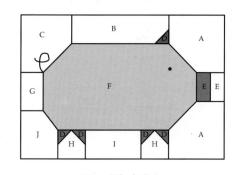

Piggy Block Going
Make 16 (flip pattern)

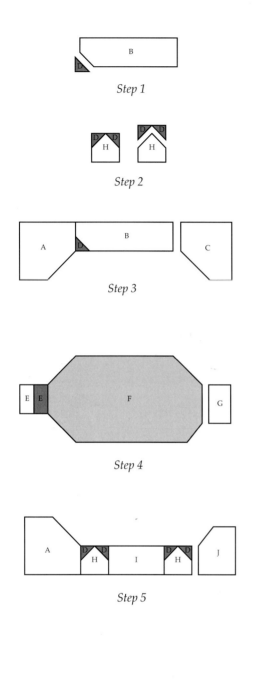

Step 1

Step 2

Step 3

Step 4

Step 5

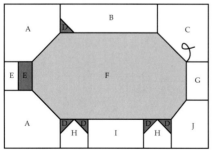

Step 6–7

Backing: 2—63″ (160 cm) lengths
Batting: 63″×79″ (160 cm×200.6 cm)
Binding (dark green): 5—2½″ (6.4 cm) strips × width of fabric

CONSTRUCTING THE BLOCKS

You will need thirty-two completed pig blocks for this quilt top. Half of these can be cut in reverse, as ours are, so that half the pigs are high-tailing it for home while the other half are headed for market. Press all seams as you go.

1. Join D (ear) to B (background).
2. Join 2 Ds (feet) to an H. Repeat.
3. Then join A to D-B. Add C to form the top band.
4. Next add background E to E (nose), to F (pig body), to G to form the middle band.
5. Last join A to D-H-D, to I, to D-H-D, to J.
6. Join the units formed in steps 3–5 to complete the block.
7. Add tails to the pigs by drawing a length of pearl cotton through the back of the fabric. Touch the end with Fray Check™ to prevent raveling. Make the cotton into a curling tail and tack it in place using a couching stitch. Just before reaching the end of the couching line, trim any excess length from the pearl cotton, touch with Fray Check,™ and complete the stitching. See page 88, Linear Details, for more detailed directions on couching.
8. Eyes can be cut from Ultra Suede® or similar suedelike, nonwoven material. Rinse this material in warm water and iron dry to avoid any later possiblity of a color running. Use a paper punch to cut the small circles. Because the suede is thick, some circles may not cut completely (or some punches will rebel). On those, the punch will mark the circle and you can easily trim around it with embroidery scissors. Then use tiny whip or catch stitches to secure the eye in place. Once eyes are added, the piggies take on a new life!

ASSEMBLING THE QUILT TOP

1. When all blocks are finished, press and join them in rows of 4 across and 8 down, alternating the direction of the pigs by rows. Match all corners and check to be sure the rows are identical in length.
2. Blocks can be joined by machine sewing or by hand, as ours are.

ADDING BORDERS

1. Add the longer white borders to the two sides of the quilt and trim ends.

2. Sew a white square to one end of the top border. Add to quilt, aligning square with the edge of side border. Sew to within 8″ (20.3 cm) of end. Measure the remaining border to the end, allowing for ¼″ (6 mm) seam allowance, trim and add second square. Finish sewing the border to the quilt top. Repeat for bottom border.

3. Repeat the same process for the second (pink) and third (green) borders. This will give you squares set into each corner.

BACKING

1. Remove selvages and then join the two 62″ (157.5 cm) lengths of backing fabric. The seam will go across the back of the quilt. The backing will extend about 15″ (38.1 cm) past the top or bottom edge of the quilt top. Trim to allow 2″ (5.1 cm) at each edge of the quilt.

2. Place backing, batting, and quilt top together according to our directions on page 117.

QUILTING

Follow the general directions on page 118. Pink quilting threads were used on areas of pink and white in both the borders and the pigs while green thread was used on the green fabrics.

1. In the white borders, quilt 2 long straight lines that parallel each of the seamlines at ¼″ (6 mm). In the top and bottom borders, lettering will fill the remaining space. In the side borders, fill the space with a third line of quilting. Use the photograph as a guide.

2. In the top and bottom white borders, quilt the familiar words of "This little piggy" in higgledy-piggledy fashion. You can find this pattern in the back of the book. You will need to repeat the pattern of the initial phrase in order to make the entire verse. The top white border reads:

"This little piggy went to market . . . this little piggy stayed home . . ."

The bottom border reads:

"This little piggy had roast beef . . . this little piggy had none." Use a quilting thread that contrasts in color to make the lettering visible in the white borders. A bright pink spells out our singsong verse.

3. In the pink border, two lines of quilting divide the space evenly.

4. In the final border of green, our quilting does an "about face" and heads off in the other direction. These crosswise lines are 1" (2.5 cm) apart and butt into the line of stitches near the seamline.

5. Within each block, quilting stitches parallel the seamlines of the pigs and the block itself. Each pig has a line of quilting around both its inside and outside, ¼" (6 mm) from the seams. The printed spots and large polka dots are outlined in quilting. When there are no large spots to quilt around (as on solid-colored or microdotted fabrics) create quilted spots of similar shapes.

BINDING

Join the binding strips with diagonal seams. This binding finishes at ½" (13 mm) and has mitered corners. See general directions for binding on page 120.

THE FINAL TOUCH

Hold up your chinny-chin-chin and sign your quilt before some Big Bad Wolf comes to huff and puff and blow your quilt into the next county. Place your own name and the date into the white side borders, using the block letters from "This little piggy."

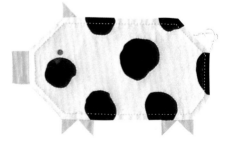

NAP PADS

Almost every preschooler carries a bundle or blanket to school for what is euphemistically called "rest time." Kindergarten kids need some kind of pad to lie down on for a quiet period. When that scheduled hour arrives, thumbs seek their old haunts and the comfort of a familiar quilt is an invitation to drowsy calm.

Nap pads are great at home, too. A special blanket reserved just for nap time or resting makes the whole prospect of napping a little more inviting. The nap pad should be small enough for a child to tote about easily and should be both washable and durable. Most kids will readily curl up on a chair or under a table with a favorite cover-up.

A make-believe friend, appliquéd on a quilt, gives the child company during rest time. Then it can be the friend who needs the rest and the child who provides the company. We have made two friends on our nap pads, a princess and a dog. Kids respond to both with an abundance of enthusiasm, and several small fry have kindly offered to "take care" of these for me.

We like nap pads that prompt a child's inclination to rest. And perhaps we need to take a quick look at our own inclinations in making them. These are the quilts we give to kids to use, play with, or roll in. If the child wants to use the quilt to wrap the dog or wishes to drag it under the table or out on the porch, that should be OK. Kids are rarely concerned if cookie crumbs or stickiness from their peanut butter and jelly sandwich cling to their fingers as they reach for their quilts. Once given to the child, a quilt should really be hers or his—not to look at or hang on the wall or keep, but to really use. And that's not always easy. It is hard to give away things we have made without having some invisible strings attached. On occasion, we don't even know the strings are there until some incident suddenly makes us conscious of them. As orange juice soaks quickly into your quilting stitches, a slight twang reverberates from those strings. A youngster, stepping on one corner of your magnificent creation and simultaneously tugging at the other, may cause dismay as a little popping sound lets you know a stitch has given way.

So make a nap pad that you are willing to see used. Then enjoy watching the process. Because they are small and easily carried, these quilts are going to be favorites. Probably the best thing that can happen to a nap pad is for it to get totally used up, worn out, and loved to the end.

Both of our nap pads are appliquéd; one by hand and one by machine. One is tied and the other is machine quilted.

Cotton velveteen's luxurious texture makes this princess an especially huggable one. The appliqués are of cotton and are hand sewn. Because of the velveteen's pile, fabrics placed on it tend to shift easily during appliqué. Pinning or basting will help, and our method of faced appliqué keeps any shifting to a minimum. But be prepared for your princess to have a slight list to the right or left. Remain flexible. It is not essential that the princess be perfectly symmetrical.

Little girls who love fairy tales will find the princess a perfect napping companion. If you like the idea of this quilt, but the youngster you have in mind isn't enamored of princesses, simply scatter stars over the velveteen sky. The Big Dipper or Ursa Minor could become the central motif for your starry design. The pad is wide enough to fold over for cover, and it is thick and puffy between the ties. Remember that kids aren't the only ones who take naps.

A portrait of our princess, with her feet firmly planted and toes primly pointing to the east and west, appears on page 74.

Read Before Starting Your Quilt on page 15.

Finished size: 48″ × 62″ (121.9 cm × 157.5 cm)

YARDAGE

Note: Based on 40″ width for velveteen, 45″ for other fabric.

Background (brown velveteen): 1⅓ yards (122 cm)
Note: Remember that velveteen appears to change color as the nap changes.
Skirt, stars, lips (red cotton): ½ yard (46 cm)
Petticoat scallops (lavender): 3″ strip (7.6 cm)
Apron (green polka dot): ⅓ yard (31 cm)

Designed and tied by Jean Ray Laury, assembled by Bea Slater

Blouse (dark green): 5″ × 5½″ (12.7 cm × 14 cm)

Sleeves, shoes (blue): ¼ yard (23 cm)

Arms, neck, face, features, hair, stars, belt (assorted colors): scraps

Crown (silver lamé): 4″ × 5½″ (10.2 cm × 14 cm)

Lace edging: 26″ (66 cm)

Nonfusible interfacing (lightweight, nonwoven): 1½ yards, 18″ wide (137 cm, 45.7 cm wide)

Borders (red velveteen): 1 yard (91 cm), if cut on crosswise grain, 1⅓ yard (122 cm), if cut on lengthwise grain

Backing: 3 yards (274 cm)

Batting (medium to heavy weight): 52″ × 66″ (132.1 cm × 167.6 cm)

Binding (blue velveteen): 1 yard (91 cm)

Yarn for ties: 35 yards (32 m) or 2 skeins of pearl cotton

CUTTING

Note: Refer to diagrams for cutting out the large shapes. Use templates for small shapes.

Background (brown velveteen): 1 panel, 37″ × 45″ (94 cm × 114.3 cm)

Skirt (red cotton): 26½″ × 16½″ (67.3 cm × 41.9 cm)

Stars (red cotton): 4

Petticoat scallops (lavender): 3″ × 26″ (7.6 cm × 66 cm)

Apron (green polka dot): 12″ × 14½″ (30.5 cm × 36.8 cm)

Blouse (dark green): 5″ × 5½″ (12.7 cm × 14 cm)

Sleeves (blue): 2—3″ × 3½″ (7.6 cm × 8.9 cm)

Shoes (blue): 2, flip for one

Arms, neck, face, features, hair, stars, belt (assorted colors)

Note: Remember to flip the pattern for one arm.

Crown (silver lamé): 4″ × 5½″ (10.2 cm × 14 cm)

Nonfusible interfacing

To back all pattern parts that will be hand appliquéd. Cut interfacing pieces ¼″ to ½″ (6 mm to 13 mm) larger than the fabric they will back.

Borders (red velveteen)

    Sides: 2—4½″ × 47″ (11.4 cm × 119.4 cm)

    Top and bottom: 2—7½″ × 47″ (19.1 cm × 119.4 cm)

Backing: 2—54″ (137.2 cm) lengths

Batting: 52″ × 66″ (132.1 cm × 167.6 cm)

Binding (blue velveteen): 6—5″ (12.7 cm) strips × width of fabric

ASSEMBLING THE QUILT TOP

Prepare the fabric for faced-appliqué by backing each cut part with a piece of interfacing cut slightly larger than the pattern. To back the fabric, place right side of fabric to facing. Sew around the entire edge on the seamline. Cut away excess, trim corners, and clip inside curves. Then cut a slit in the facing at center back, and turn the entire piece right side out. Press carefully so that none of the interfacing shows. This provides a finished edge, which makes the appliqué much easier to handle, particularly on velveteen.

You do not need to create a finished edge on any piece that will be overlapped, as the raw edge will be flatter. For example, the neck will be covered by both the head and blouse. Finish the neck only at the side edges; leave the top and bottom raw. Dashed lines on the patterns show which edges to leave unsewn when adding interfacing. *Note:* If you find it difficult to keep the interfacing from occasionally peeking out at the edges, you can baste the edges (before appliqué) to eliminate the problem. Or, each fabric can be self-backed. That is, on a red star, use a matching piece of red fabric instead of interfacing. It will be slightly heavier but no more difficult to sew; however, you will need to double the amount of appliqué fabric.

1. As the velveteen tends to "shed" on the cut edges, turn under a small hem on the background piece and baste it in place. Place the large brown background piece on a flat surface so that the various parts of the princess can be placed on top. Complete the appliqué before you add any borders.

2. Templates are provided for many cut shapes. You will need to cut paper patterns for others, according to our diagrams and directions. Cutting your own patterns for the princess will be simpler than you imagine. You will need some butcher paper or any similar plain white paper. Tape smaller sheets together if necessary. Newspaper will work but care must be taken not to transfer printing ink to your fabric. All patterns and templates include a ¼" (6 mm) seam allowance.

Although the directions call for pinning all pieces in place, you may want to baste the parts as well.

3. For the skirt pattern, cut a paper to 26½" × 16½" (67.3 cm × 41.9 cm). Fold the paper in half (lengthwise) so that the 16½" (41.9 cm) edges are folded together. See diagram. Put the fold at your left. Mark a spot 3" (7.6 cm) from the fold at the top edge. Then draw a full round curved line from the lower right hand corner to the pencil mark at the top. This will give you more or less a half circle. Cut the paper, then unfold it and check the shape. Use the pattern to cut out the red skirt.

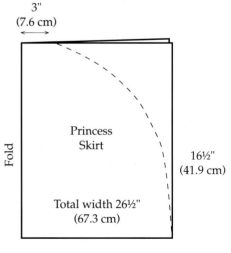

3"
(7.6 cm)

Fold

Princess
Skirt

16½"
(41.9 cm)

Total width 26½"
(67.3 cm)

Step 3

4. Line, turn, and then place the skirt on the brown background fabric, 7" (17.8 cm) from the bottom cut edge and centered side to side. Pin in place.

5. To make the scallops (or petticoat), fold the lavender piece in half lengthwise. Pin or crease that halfway spot to mark it. Fold each side in half and mark again. Then fold and mark each section once more. You will have eight sections in all. Draw curves from point to point; you can use any small dish or glass to guide your curve. The circle should be about 3" (7.6 cm) in diameter. See diagram. Back the scallops with interfacing, leaving the long top edge open. Clip curves, turn, and press. Pin this band so that the open edge tucks under the skirt.

6. Lace can be inserted at the lower edge of the skirt with the scallops, or it can be added afterward.

7. The apron pattern is made in the same way as the skirt. Cut a rectangle of paper 14½" × 12½" (36.8 cm × 31.8 cm). Fold in half lengthwise so the 14½" (36.8 cm) edges are together, and place the fold at your left. Mark a spot 2½" (6.4 cm) from the fold at top. Draw a curved line from the lower right corner to the mark at the top. Cut. Open to check shape, and cut your fabric. Back with interfacing, leaving the top end open, and pin to skirt letting raw edges meet at top. Tuck a bit of lace under the lower edge of the apron now, or add it on top later.

8. The blouse is a 5" × 5½" (12.7 cm × 14 cm) rectangle. With the narrower dimension at the top, drop ¼" (6 mm) at each shoulder to make a slight curve from shoulder to shoulder. Line, leaving bottom edge open as it will be covered. Pin blouse in place with raw lower edge within ½" (13 mm) of apron top.

9. Cut sleeves from the 3" × 3½" (7.6 cm × 8.9 cm) rectangles. Curve 2 corners and keep 2 of them squared. See the diagram. Line. The edge that slips under the blouse is left open. Pin these in place, slipping raw edge under blouse.

10. Cut belt 1½" × 5" (3.8 cm × 12.7 cm). Finish on all sides.

11. Prepare the crown; cut a rectangle 4" × 5½" (10.2 cm × 14 cm). Fold longer edge in half to mark center point. Fold each side in half again and mark. Cut a large "V" from center fold to one edge, making it about 2" (5.1 cm) deep. See diagram. Repeat for second side. Line, sewing on all edges as crown will overlap hair.

12. Cut all remaining patterns from templates and be sure that all shapes are lined, turned, and pressed.

13. Pin the rest of the pieces in place in this order: shoes (centered, 4" [10.2 cm] apart and 4½" [11.4 cm] from bottom edge; tuck tops of shoes under petticoat), belt (overlap blouse and apron), arms (slip

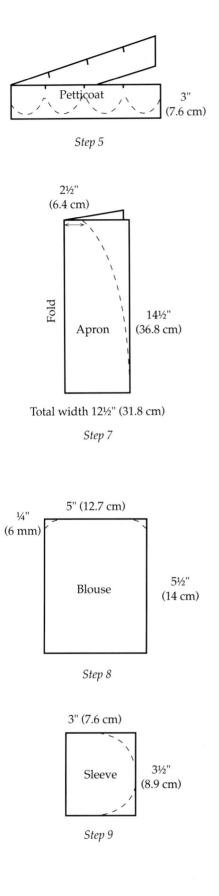

Petticoat — 3" (7.6 cm)

Step 5

2½" (6.4 cm)

Fold

Apron — 14½" (36.8 cm)

Total width 12½" (31.8 cm)

Step 7

5" (12.7 cm)

¼" (6 mm)

Blouse — 5½" (14 cm)

Step 8

3" (7.6 cm)

Sleeve — 3½" (8.9 cm)

Step 9

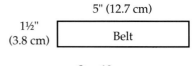

5" (12.7 cm)

1½"
(3.8 cm)   Belt

Step 10

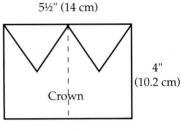

5½" (14 cm)

4"
(10.2 cm)

Crown

Step 11

raw edges under sleeves and overlap skirt with hands), neck (slip edge under blouse), hair, face (place on top of hair and overlap neck), bangs, crown, and features. Finally, scatter all stars over the background.

14. Appliqué all pieces in place by hand, using thread that matches the color of the fabric being appliquéd.

15. Remove any basting.

ADDING BORDERS

1. Add the narrow red borders to the sides of the quilt after removing any basting you may have used on the background edges.

2. Then add the wide top and bottom borders to complete the quilt top.

BACKING

For the backing, join the two lengths of material after cutting away the selvages. Slide the excess to either top or bottom and trim, leaving 2″ (5.1 cm) at each edge. You will have one horizontal seam across the back of the quilt.

QUILTING

To prepare the layers, read our general directions on page 117. Directions for tying follow.

1. Stack the backing fabric, a bonded batt, and the quilt top. You may wish to use a thicker-than-normal batt because the nap pad will be used on the floor. The backing should extend 2″ to 3″ (5.1 cm to 7.6 cm) beyond the cut edge of the quilt.

2. Baste the layers together in a grid with the basted lines no more than 3″ to 4″ (7.6 cm to 10.2 cm) apart.

3. Fold backing over raw edges of the quilt top, covering excess batting. Baste to keep the loose batting from catching.

4. To mark the exact locations for the ties at 3″ (7.6 cm) intervals, measure on the front side of the quilt. Place a pin straight down through the layers. Mark the front and back points with a pencil or tailor's chalk. Remove pins. A little shifting of the tie locations will avoid having ties in the middle of the princess's face or directly on stitched appliqué lines.

5. Tie the quilt, using yarn or cord. Wool or cotton, which tend to tighten with use or with washing, are preferrable. Synthetic yarns tend to work loose. The princess is tied on the back of the quilt. This leaves a ¼″ (6 mm) stitch of the red yarn showing on the front. In the side borders, a ½″ (13 mm) space remains next to each seamline with two rows of ties in between. In the top and bottom borders, the same ½" (13 mm) interval is left, with 3 rows of ties between. The rest of the top is divided into a 3" (7.6 cm) grid.

6. You can speed up the tying process by taking continuous stitches from one marked point to the next, moving in a line across the quilt. Make sure you leave ample yarn to tie the knots easily. Then go back to clip the yarn or cord and tie the knots. Trim the ties to ¾" (19 mm). Trim the excess backing and batting to extend 2" (5.1 cm) beyond the edge of the quilt top.

BINDING

Velveteen is somewhat bulkier than most fabrics, so this binding is measured and sewn in a different way. Read our general directions on page 120. Instead of the double-thick binding usually used, this binding is single fold.

1. Piece the 5" (12.7 cm) wide lengths of the binding with diagonal seams, and cut into 2 strips 62" (157.5 cm) long and 2 strips 52" (132.1 cm) long.

2. Place the long bindings, face side down, on the sides of the quilt top. The raw edges of binding will align with the raw edges of the quilt; the batting and backing will extend beyond. Pin or baste. Sew.

3. Fold the binding over to the back of the quilt and allow the extra batting to roll and fill the binding. If any areas seem to be skimpily filled, add extra batting.

4. Turn under ½" (13 mm) of the binding and slip stitch to seamline on the back of the quilt.

5. Repeat for top and bottom bindings and square the corners as on page 121.

THE FINAL TOUCH

If this quilt is to be carted off to preschool by the would-be napper, you definitely need to identify the name of the young owner. This information could be "in the stars," across the bottom of the skirt, or in a separate panel added to the back. Include your own name, and (as a precaution) your phone number . . . just in case a fellow napper borrows the nap pad and forgets where it came from.

Designed by Jean Ray Laury, assembled and quilted by Bea Slater

Any napper would rest easy under the guardianship of this watch (out) dog. He's "wired" for action, electrified and alert! The materials are sturdy, and the machine-stitched appliqué and quilting add to its durability. Wild colors seem especially appropriate for a wild dog, and this one is a great favorite of nappers young or old. Our nap pad is quilted, but it could be tied instead. See page 78, Quilting, for full tying instructions.

On the previous page, the dog bristled nicely and bared his teeth for the photographer.

Read Before Starting Your Quilt on page 15.

Finished size: 41½″ × 50″ (105.4 cm × 127 cm)

YARDAGE

Note: Heavy cottons, such as sailcloth, denim, or sport cottons will work well for large areas.

Background (blue): 1 yard (91 cm)

Flames (yellow): ⅔ yard (60 cm)

Flames (red): ⅔ yard (60 cm)

Dog head, body, legs, ear, tail (polka dot): ⅓ yard (31 cm)

Mouth (white): 3″ × 5″ (7.6 cm × 12.7 cm)

Interfacing (Wonder-Under® or similar lightweight, nonwoven, double fusible interfacing in white): 3 yards (274 cm)

Borders (green): ¾ yard (69 cm)

Backing: 1½ yards (137 cm)

Batting (medium weight): 45″ × 54″ (114.3 cm × 137.2 cm)

Binding (polka dot): 1½ yards (137.2 cm)

CUTTING

Backgound (blue): 30½″ × 34½″ (77.5 cm × 87.6 cm)

Dog (polka dot): use templates and directions

Note: Before cutting yellow, red, or polka-dot dogs, iron Wonder-Under® to the back side of the fabric.

Yellow

12 triangles

1 eye

flames, according to templates and directions

Red

11 triangles

flames, according to templates and directions

Borders (green)

Sides: 2—5″ × 36½″ (12.7 cm × 92.7 cm)

Top: 6½″ × 41½″ (16.5 cm × 105.4 cm)

Bottom: 8″ × 41½″ (20.3 cm × 105.4 cm)

Backing: Use 1½ yard (137 cm) length as is, with selvages at sides of quilt

Batting: 45″ × 54″ (114.3 cm × 137.2 cm)

Binding

Sides: 2—5½″ × 50″ (14 cm × 127 cm)

Top and bottom: 2—5½″ × 46″ (14 cm × 116.8 cm)

ASSEMBLING THE QUILT TOP

1. Apply the Wonder-Under® according to package directions to all appliqué fabrics before cutting, covering areas only slightly larger than needed.

2. Using the template for the dog's head, cut the dog out of the polka-dot material, extending the body an additional 12″ (30.5 cm) in length and maintaining the 5½″ (14 cm) width. Round off the corners.

3. Next cut ear and tail out of the polka-dot material.

4. All legs are cut from the same pattern, but vary in the angle and amount of overlap. The legs are numbered right to left. Leg 1 (the frong leg) is overlapped up to the broken line indicated on the pattern. Cut out all 4 legs.

5. Cut the teeth out of white.

6. Spread out the red fabric on a large flat area, and arrange the dog parts on it. Remove the backing from the iron-on facing on the dog parts and press to adhere all parts to the red.

7. Cut the red fabric around the dog shape, leaving 1″ to 2″ (2.5 cm to 5.1 cm) of excess fabric on all edges. Then cut these edges into

jagged flame shapes. The leg template has an example of how to cut these lines.

8. Remove backing from the red shape and adhere it to the yellow fabric. Again cut around the dog shape but allow a wider edge on the yellow. Cut it into jagged shapes.

9. Remove the backing and apply the yellow dog shape to the blue background, pressing the corners carefully to assure that they are adhered. The polka-dot tummy of the dog will be 17½″ (44.5 cm) from the cut lower edge of the blue background. The polka-dot nose will be 4½″ (11.4 cm) from the right-hand edge of the background.

10. Add the eye.

11. Machine appliqué all parts in place starting with the yellow fabric. Use matching thread color. Use a full width zigzag satin stitch, sewing according to the directions on page 85.

12. Scatter the triangles randomly over the nap pad so that the yellow ones are in the border and the red ones are on the blue background. Appliqué them in place.

ADDING BORDERS

1. Add the side green borders and trim.

2. Add top and bottom borders, using the wider border at the bottom. Square corners and trim ends.

QUILTING

Read page 117 for the general directions on stacking the backing, batting, and quilt top. Trim the excess backing and batting to extend 2″ (5.1 cm) beyond the edge of the quilt top. Read page 119 for details about machine quilting. Although a light or thin batt generally gives the best results, in this case we need a heavier filler as the nap pad will be used on the floor. A medium weight will work best, as the fat batts tend to shift under the machine quilting.

1. Outline the dog, the red flames, and the yellow flames with lines of straight machine quilting. The quilted line is taken right next to the satin-stitched lines.

2. Quilt the entire background in a grid pattern with lines 1½″ (3.8 cm) apart. The grid is placed diagonally to create a diamond pattern over the quilt. The grid does not cross over the dog or triangles but abuts the stitches that outline them. Use the photograph as a guide.

BINDING

Read the directions on binding, page 120. This quilt has a wide binding that finishes at 1¼" (3.2 cm) with squared corners. Be sure that your batting extends past the quilt top to fill the extra-wide binding.

THE FINAL TOUCH

Nap pads need to be identified with their owner's name; the more easily read the better. Perhaps you'll want to add a dog collar and stitch the napper's name there. Remember that as dogcatcher, your name should be emblazoned somewhere on this canine creation. Add the date and the name of your town or the school, too, as this is bound to be a favorite nap pad.

Having a whole crowd of people or animals take up residence on the coverlet is some kids' idea of a good time. They love crowds and faces of all kinds and want to be immersed in the center of the action. Having lots of faces staring from a quilt top is fun, but it's something seldom encountered on quilts. Most quilters think of faces as hard to do.

We've simplified these faces and designed them for versatility. You can easily alter the faces in *My Family* so that it's your own uncles, nieces, brothers, or neighbors who lodge permanently in your quilt. In the *Animal Fair*, your own favorite backyard critters can be the ones chosen to inhabit your land of counterpane.

All the quilts in this section are machine appliquéd. Sturdy durability makes them good candidates for the rough-and-tumble of a child's playroom.

MACHINE APPLIQUÉ

Two different methods of machine appliqué have been used in these quilts. Neither requires a turn-under allowance, so all templates are given in finished size. If you prefer to use hand appliqué, *add a seam allowance* to each cut edge of these templates so that raw edges can be tucked under for stitching.

Always secure starting and ending threads. Pull any loose threads through to the back and knot. Then trim the threads. Where shapes overlap, it is not necessary to knot. For example, if a face overlaps an ear, the threads of the ear stitching will be caught by stitches at the edge of the face.

PAPER BACKING

To follow the method used on *My Family* and *Animal Fair,* first baste (or use a minimum touch of a fabric glue stick) to hold the face parts in place. When a glue stick is very lightly used, fabric pieces can be shifted or changed as necessary. The appliqué of points and corners will be easier when each has been secured with the adhesive. All satin stitches should make a smooth, solid line, without the individual stitches showing (stitches are exaggerated in the diagrams).

Place a sheet of paper (inexpensive typing or copy paper will work well) under the fabric background block, next to the sewing machine feed dogs. Having the paper as a bottom layer stabilizes the fabric and gives you perfectly flat appliqué.

Machine embroidery thread, which is easy to use, gives a very smooth, professional appliqué line. Using high-quality thread will help eliminate much of the frustration of broken or frayed threads. Machine stitch, using a zigzag satin stitch on medium setting (approximately 2 to 3 mm) over exposed cut edges. Stitch through fabric layers and paper. If your paper sheet is smaller than the fabric, it may be necessary to butt a second piece of paper up against the first. Change thread color as necessary to match the color of the appliqué fabric, keeping your bobbin thread the same as your background block.

To achieve sharp points, gradually narrow your zigzag as you approach the point so the width of the zigzag does not exceed the width of the point. Sew just past the fabric point until your stitch width is 0. Lift the presser foot and pivot the fabric. Sew the remaining edge by gradually increasing the stitch width until the original setting is reached. See diagram 1. The outside stitch should be placed exactly at the edge of the fabric so that it catches all threads but does not extend beyond the material.

For smooth corners, satin stitch one edge all the way to the next cut edge. See diagram 2. Stop with the needle in the fabric at the raw edge. Pivot to change directions, and stitch over the end of the last line of stitching to create a smooth corner. When possible, start and stop stitching on a straight part of the shape. As you complete the shape it will be easier to line up the ending stitches with the beginning stitches, thus securing the first stitches and making a smooth line.

Circles require more practice. For small circles, use a narrow satin stitch. Several of the eyes in these quilts are cut from polka-dot fabric. For example, a blue dot on white fabric could be cut so that, when appliquéd, there is a blue circle surrounded by a white circle. This avoids the appliqué of tiny circles, which are more difficult to keep perfectly round.

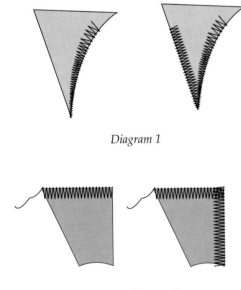

Diagram 1

Diagram 2

A small extension, generally ¼″ (6 mm), has been added to some of the pattern pieces where overlap is important. For example, to add ears, slip them under the head shape. This is much easier than butting cut edges together and trying to catch both raw edges under the satin stitch.

When a block is complete, gently tear away the paper and press the block. If you find the paper is difficult to pull away, spray it lightly with water before pulling. Then pin the portrait up on the wall. As you glance at it from time to time, ideas for variations will pop into your mind. Experiment with the features, and play with the faces. It's lots of fun and you'll come up with some variations you'll want to include in your quilt.

ADHESIVE LINING

Circus Clowns was appliquéd using a different method. The fabric was backed with Wonder-Under®, a lightweight material that has two fusible sides, before the appliqué pieces were cut. Follow the directions that come with this double-adhesive backing, available at quilt or fabric shops. Once the fusible material is pressed with an iron onto the appliqué piece, the paperlike backing is peeled away and the piece can then be pressed onto the background block. This adds body and a slight stiffness. It also makes the material easier to handle and greatly simplifies the machine appliqué stitching. The machine satin stitch is then used to cover each exposed raw edge, using a medium setting of about 3 mm.

Either of the methods described, paper-backing or adhesive lining, can be used successfully on any of these quilts. When blocks are complete, they should be pressed well.

HAND APPLIQUÉ

To hand appliqué, add a ¼″ (6 mm) turn-under allowance (or less) at each cut edge. Place the appliqué on the background block, aligning shapes according to finished sizes. It will be necessary, for example, to tuck ears under the face shape so that the overlap line is even with the finished line (not the cut line) of the face. Pin the shapes in place and appliqué underlying ones first: sew neck, overlap with shoulders. Ears should be appliquéd before the face, with features last. Use any preferred hand appliqué method, turning under the seam allowance and stitching at the outside edge. It will not be necessary to appliqué any area that is overlapped by another. For example, only the sides of the neck need to be stitched down. Top and bottom edges are covered by the face and shoulders in most of the blocks.

LINEAR DETAILS

All lines and details (animal whiskers, mouths, stems) can be embroidered either by machine or by hand. Using pearl cotton you can draw or place the lines on the fabric, then machine zigzag them in place. This is often referred to as couching.

To machine sew the pearl cotton onto your block, cut a length of the cotton or yarn. A piece about 20″ (50.8 cm) long is easier to handle than a number of small pieces trimmed to the exact sizes needed (the end can be clipped off after sewing). Apply Fray Check™ to one end of the cotton and start the stitching at that end. A small bar tack will secure it. (Take three or four stitches in one spot, forming a short bar, before starting the zigzag. Tie ends of threads on back.) When you have completed the line of detail, clip off any excess cord and stitch over the clipped end, finishing with Fray Check™ and another bar tack. See diagram 3. The longer piece of cord aids you in guiding it through the machine. It is difficult to hold a short piece in place with any accuracy.

Machine satin stitches in medium width can also be used to create the linear details, eliminating the pearl cotton or cord. Sketch the line with a basting stitch, sewn either by hand or machine. Then satin stitch over the basting line. If this tight stitching distorts the background block slightly, stretch the area to be stitched in an embroidery hoop. Place the larger half of the hoop on your work surface, then center the area to be sewn, right side up, over it. Press the smaller, inner hoop on top. That will keep the fabric down flat on the surface of the sewing machine. Lift the presser foot and tilt the hoop if necessary to ease it under the needle. Slip a sheet of paper under the fabric to help prevent any distortion from the close stitches.

For hand sewing, use a couching stitch as shown in diagram 4. To do this, thread the cord on a large-eyed needle and draw it through from the back. Arrange the cord on top of the fabric to form the line you want. Then pull a thread of matching color through from the back right next to the cord. Secure the thread with a small knot, and tack the cord in place. Use a series of small overcast stitches to couch the cord in place. Pull the cord fairly taut so that it creates a smooth line. When you near the end of the line, draw the cord, then the tacking thread, through to the back and secure each. Embroidery floss, pearl cotton, cord, or crochet thread will all work satisfactorily. If you are uncertain as to colorfastness, be sure to rinse the cord in hot water and iron it dry.

Diagram 3
Machine couching

Diagram 4
Hand couching

Designed by Jean Ray Laury, assembled and quilted by Susan Smeltzer

MY FAMILY

Here's a perfect way to make a "family album" quilt. You can depict each of your relatives on a separate colorful appliqué block. We have included patterns for all twenty-two faces shown here. General directions are given for completing one face, and the remaining portraits can be made following those same steps.

If you prefer to design your own faces, first select the most appropriate face shape. Is your portrait of someone with a round face? a long face? a bald head? a square jaw? Next select your subject's most notable facial characteristic . . . a mustache, glasses, long nose, heavy eyebrows, round cheeks, big eyes, long hair, and so on. Find the patterns closest to your needs, then trace or copy them. Modify them or cut new paper patterns as necessary. To do this, place the patterns for the hair, eyes, or whatever on the fabric face to get an impression of how they'll work. Or use small scraps of fabric to try different shapes and colors for the features. Having a snapshot to work from may make it easier to achieve a likeness. You'll be surprised how many of these faces already resemble your relatives!

Making these "album" quilts is great fun! You may wish to get your whole family involved . . . or you may wish to keep this portrait project all to yourself. Consider doing the faces of members of your quilting group, your son's ball team, or a Brownie troop. Characters from a child's favorite story or your own favorite historical characters offer endless variations. Your neighbors, your in-laws, and your office-mates are all fair game.

Read Before Starting Your Quilt on page 15.

Finished size: 61½″ × 86½″ (156.2 cm × 219.7 cm)
Finished size of blocks: 9½″ × 9½″ (24.1 cm × 24.1 cm)
Number of blocks: 22
Blocks set: 4 × 6 with a name panel

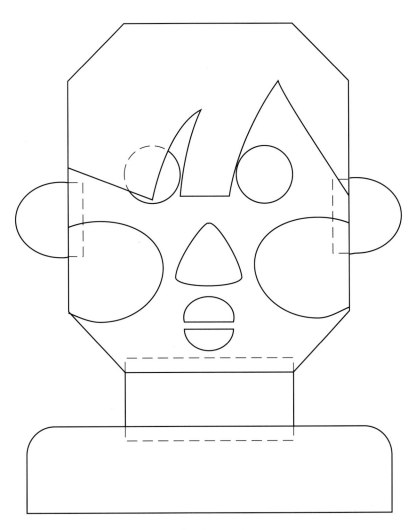

My Family Row 1–1
Assembly diagram

YARDAGE

Note: Allow additional fabric when using assorted colors, as the cutting is less efficient than when you use a single color.

Background blocks: 1¾ yards (160 cm), if all are one color, or ⅓ yard (31 cm) each of 6 different colors or 10½″ × 10½″ (26.7 cm × 26.7 cm) each color

Faces: ⅔ yard (61 cm) or 22 rectangles 5″ × 6″ (12.7 cm × 15.2 cm)

Note: Use assorted colors and patterns for faces. Include some prints, polka dots, or pale patterns as these will sometimes give you just the right skin tone.

Features and lettering: Small amounts of assorted colors.

Sashing (beige): 1 yard (91 cm)

Sashing, border, binding (red): 2¼ yards (206 cm)

Borders (blue): 2¾ yards (251 cm)

Backing: 3¾ yards (343 cm)

Batting: 66″ × 91″ (167.6 cm × 231.1 cm)

CUTTING

Note: Read directions for assembling portraits before cutting.

Measurements include seam allowance except for those areas to be machine appliquéd (the faces). If you wish to hand appliqué, be sure to add a ¼" (6 mm) turn-under allowance to all cut edges. All binding strips and long sashings include a 2" (5.1 cm) extra allowance, to be trimmed after sewing.

Background blocks (assorted colors): 22—10"×10" (25.4 cm×25.4 cm)

Title panel: 1—10"×22½" (25.4 cm×57.2 cm)

Faces (assorted colors): 22—5"×6" (12.7 cm×15.2 cm)

Features (assorted colors): as each face dictates

Letters (assorted colors)

"m" and "y"	2 each
other letters	1 each

Note: You may prefer to use the child's name, your family name, or another title to identify the group you are depicting.

Sashings (beige)

> **Sides:** 46—1¼"×10" (3.2 cm×25.4 cm)
> **Top and bottom:** 44—1¼"×11½" (3.2 cm×29.2 cm)
> **Title panel:** 2—1¼"×24" (3.2 cm×61 cm)

Note: Cut these in the following order.

Binding (red): 4—2½" (6.2 cm) strips × *length* of fabric

Borders (red)

> **Sides:** 2—2"×76" (5.1 cm×193 cm)
> **Top and bottom:** 2—2"×54" (5.1 cm×137.2 cm)

Sashing (red)

> **Long:** 5—2"×51" (5.1 cm×129.5 cm)
> **Short:** 17—2"×11½" (5.1 cm×29.2 cm)

Borders (blue)

> **Sides:** 2—5"×88" (12.7 cm×223.5 cm)
> **Top and bottom:** 2—5"×54" (12.7 cm×137.2 cm)

Backing: 2—66" (167.6 cm) lengths

Batting: 66"×91" (167.6 cm×231.1 cm)

CONSTRUCTING THE PORTRAITS

To complete your personalized portrait block, follow these general directions. The position of each block is identified by row and by position in the row. For example, 4-3 is the fourth row down, third from the left—the baby.

1. To center portraits, fold backgrounds, shoulders, and faces in half. Crease on the fold lines. Use the fold lines as guides to place shoulders, faces, and features. Align the cut edge of shoulders with

the bottom of the background block, then work upward to the neck or collar and face.

2. Where pieces overlap, tuck one shape under another, as the ears under the head. Usually the neck is tucked under the face, but occasionally a collar is placed over the face.

3. Baste the pieces in place or touch each lightly with a glue stick to keep the pieces from moving during appliqué. Appliqué all portraits with machine satin stitching to the backing squares. Use thread colors that match or blend except where a line is meant to stand out, as with a stitched mouth. Where shapes overlap, sew the bottom layer first so that the raw edges of unsewn areas will be covered by the overlapping pieces. Overlap should be ¼" (6 mm) or to the broken line on the pattern. Sew in this order: neck before shoulders, ears before face, features and hair last. Appliqué the larger shapes first, working down to the smaller ones. Sew the larger circle of an eye before the smaller one. For directions on the appliqué stitch, see page 85.

4. For linear details on eyeglasses or earrings and a few of the mouths, use a wide satin stitch to create the drawn line on the fabric.

5. Repeat for all blocks. Press each block carefully and firmly.

You'll enjoy using these patterns, but you will enjoy making your own portraits of friends and family even more. Any of these templates can be altered slightly, or combine the templates in new ways to create faces of your own.

CONSTRUCTING THE NAME PANEL

Appliqué the name panel by arranging the letters in a higgledy-piggledy pattern. This is not only decorative and informal, but it avoids the necessity of perfect spacing and alignment of letters, which may be difficult if you are new to machine appliqué. Touch each letter lightly on the reverse side with a fabric glue stick, making sure corners and points are secured. Then satin stitch the letters in place, matching top thread to the fabric color and bobbin thread to background color.

ASSEMBLING THE QUILT TOP

1. Sew short beige sashings to both *sides* of each block. Place a sashing strip face down on a finished block, aligning raw edges and matching corners. Pin and join with a straight stitch, using thread that matches the background color.

2. Sew the longer beige sashings to the top and bottom of each block. Let the seamline cross the seamlines of the side sashings. Blocks will be square.

3. Sew short beige sashings to each end of the rectangular title panel block. Then add the longest beige sashings at top and bottom. *Note:* The photograph indicates the piecing arrangement and shows the finished blocks with sashes and borders.

4. Place finished blocks on a large surface to determine the final arrangement. Keep them in rows of 4 across. Make a total of 6 rows. When you finalize the arrangement, pin numbers to the blocks to help retain their order (and your sanity). Remember that 2 blocks are eliminated in the top row to make room for the name panel.

5. Join the blocks for row 1. Sew a short red sashing to each short side of the title panel. Then add blocks 1 and 4 to the title panel, making up a horizontal row.

6. In row 2, join the 4 blocks with 3 red sashings between them.

7. Repeat for all remaining rows.

8. Use the five 51″ (129.5 cm) red sashings between the 6 rows of blocks (start between rows 1 and 2). Place rows of blocks and sashings so that right sides are facing and raw edges are together. Always start at the same side to measure so that the blocks in adjoining rows are accurately aligned. Trim the raw ends of the sashing strips.

BORDERS

1. Add a 76″ (193 cm) red border at each of the sides of the quilt top, aligning raw edges. Trim and press.

2. Add a 54″ (137.2 cm) red border at top and bottom. Trim and press.

3. Add the 2 short blue borders to the top and bottom of the quilt, again matching raw edges with right sides together. Stitch carefully, press, and trim ends. Finally, repeat for the long blue borders at the sides.

BACKING

1. Remove selvages from the backing fabric and join the 2 lengths of fabric. The backing will have one horizontal seam.

2. Trim the backing to allow an excess of 2″ (5.1 cm) at each edge. This excess is needed during the quilting.

3. Select a bonded batt, or one that will minimize any shifting during washing. This quilt is only outline quilted, which leaves spaces of several inches in some of the blocks.

4. Stack the quilt top, backing, and batting as described in the general directions on page 117.

QUILTING

1. *My Family* has been machine quilted with a straight stitch. Cotton thread was used on the bobbin with clear nylon thread through the needle. Use a walking foot (or quilting foot) on your machine, and follow each seamline of the quilt, stitching "in the ditch" on all sashings, borders, and blocks.

2. Remove the walking foot to freehand outline each head, taking stitches as close as possible to the appliqué. Follow the contour of each figure, starting with the shoulder and moving up and around the head, ending at the bottom of the opposite shoulder.

3. Quilt the blue border with diagonal lines 2″ (5.1 cm) apart. Start at the center of one side, making a right angle as shown in the photograph on page 89. The right angle point of the triangle should touch the inside edge of the red border. The parallel diagonal lines will continue down the side of the quilt. Repeat for second side. A similar right-angle corner is placed at the center top and bottom. Lines should meet at the corners to make a final diagonal line. *Note:* Because of variations in seam widths or sewing style, not all quilts will be precisely the same size. By working from the center of each side you can determine how your corners are going to work out. If the spacing needs to be adjusted, that can easily be accomplished at the corners where the last lines can be moved slightly in either direction.

BINDING

The sashing color is repeated in our bright red binding, which finishes at ½″ (13 mm). Join the strips with diagonal seams. Follow general directions on page 120 for adding the bindings. The corners are mitered.

THE FINAL TOUCH

Did you include your own portrait in the quilt? That would be a perfect place to sign and date your work. If you are not included, consider sewing a self-portrait for the back of the quilt, where you can add all the pertinent details.

CIRCUS CLOWNS

Clowns evoke our most nostalgic reminiscences of childhood. Their garish colors, their absurd and unpredictable behavior, and the laughter they invite all prompt our longing for circus days.

Kids fall into fits of giggles over clowns. They delight in seeing grown-ups who don't *act* like grown-ups. What we capture in our comical pictures of clowns is the extravagant absurdity of their looks. And they *do* look funny with their exaggerated eyes, add-on noses, and hats. But the clown portraits amuse us most of all because we associate the funny faces with their high spirits and their high jinks.

Here is a cheerful quilt over which clown after clown cavorts. It is as bright and breezy as a quilt can be. Although only two different clown-face patterns are used, the hats can be reversed to suggest greater variety. The overall use of polka dots gives a confetti-like pattern, while stripes add to the activity.

Our clowns have put on big grins for the photograph on the next page.

Read Before Starting Your Quilt on page 15.

Finished size: 66½″ × 79″ (168.9 cm × 200.7 cm)
Finished size of blocks: 9½″ × 9½″ (24.1 cm × 24.1 cm)
Number of blocks: 20 (9 of Clown A; 11 of Clown B)
Blocks set: 4 × 5

YARDAGE

Background blocks
    Dark polka dot: 1 yard (91 cm)
    Light polka dot: 1 yard (91 cm)
    Note: For a variety of colors, allow a 10″ square for each.

Designed by Jean Ray Laury, assembled and quilted by Judy DeRouchey

Sashing and squares

    Red: 1 yard (91 cm)

    White: 1 yard (91 cm)

Face colors: ½ yard (46 cm)

Shirts and collars: ½ yard (46 cm)

Hats for Clown A: ⅓ yard (31 cm)

    for Clown B: ¼ yard (23 cm)

Features: Assorted colors and patterns. Select your most colorful scraps, or buy ¼ yard (23 cm) of 4 or 5 additional colors. Total needed per clown, about 12″ × 12″ (30.5 cm × 30.5 cm).

Interfacing: 2½ yards (227 cm) double-faced, iron-on, nonwoven, such as Wonder-Under®

Border (striped): ⅔ yard (61 cm)

Border (navy): 2 yards (183 cm)

Backing: 4⅔ yards (426 cm)

Batting: 71″ × 84″ (180.3 cm × 213.4 cm)

Binding (striped, cut on diagonal): 1 yard (91 cm)

CUTTING

Background blocks

    Light (polka dots): 10—10″ × 10″ (25.4 cm × 25.4 cm)

    Dark (polka dots): 10—10″ × 10″ (25.4 cm × 25.4 cm)

    or use mixed colors to total 20 squares.

Clown A (12 templates): 9 each

Clown B (13 templates): 11 each

Cut clowns from colors and patterns. (Back these with the double-faced interfacing before cutting, following interfacing directions.) *Note:* Cut just one of each pattern piece for each clown except where 2 are indicated on the templates. For ears and hair, cut a left and right by flipping the pattern for the second piece.

Sashing strips and squares

    Strips (red): 49—2″ × 10″ (5.1 cm × 25.4 cm)

    Strips (white): 49—2″ × 10″ (5.1 cm × 25.4 cm)

    Squares (red): 60—2″ × 2″ (5.1 cm × 5.1 cm)

    Squares (white): 60—2″ × 2″ (5.1 cm × 5.1 cm)

First Border

    Sides (striped, cut crosswise): 2—2¾″ × 67½″ (7 cm × 171.5 cm)

    Top and bottom (striped, cut crosswise): 2—2¾″ × 55½″ (7 cm × 141 cm)

    Border squares (red): 4—2¾″ × 2¾″ (7 cm × 7 cm)

Second border

    Sides (navy): 2—4½″ × 72½″ (11.4 cm × 184.2 cm)

    Top and bottom (navy): 2—4½″ × 59″ (11.4 cm × 149.9 cm)

Border squares (red): 4—4½″ × 4½″ (11.4 cm × 11.4 cm)
Backing: 2—84″ (213.4 cm) lengths
Batting: 71″ × 84″ (180.3 cm × 213.4 cm)
Binding: 2½″ (6.4 cm) strips, cut on bias

CONSTRUCTING THE BLOCKS

1. Arrange face parts for the clown blocks as shown in the diagram, removing the paper backing from each as positions are determined. Although there are just 2 face patterns, by using many colors and by reversing the hats, you can create the illusion of greater variety. Tilt the flower to the left on one block and to the right on the next. The tassled hat can also swing from side to side. Some pattern pieces are to be slipped under adjacent shapes, and a broken line on the template indicates the extent of the tuck. Some pieces will be stacked, as with the circle of the eye, which goes on top of a triangle on top of a face.

2. When the arrangement is final, press with an iron to fuse fabrics in place, following instructions that come with the interfacing. This bonds the fabrics firmly and simplifies the sewing as it secures the many small shapes and gives extra body to the fabric.

3. Stitch all raw edges with a smooth satin stitch in a medium width, about 3 mm. Change thread colors to match pattern parts, or do all the appliqué with black thread, as we did on our clowns. Press the finished blocks.

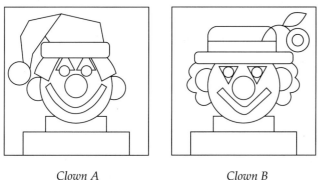

Clown A   *Clown B*

Step 1

ASSEMBLING THE QUILT TOP

The blocks are now ready for the addition of the sashings. Dark blocks will have white sashings with red corner squares. Light blocks will have red sashings with white corner squares.

1. Add sashings to both left and right sides of each block first.

2. Add corner squares to each end of the top and bottom sashings.

3. Add these sashings to the top and bottom edges of the blocks, matching seams carefully, to complete squares. Each block will be "framed" as in the diagram.

4. When all sashings are completed, make a final arrangement of the blocks, alternating sashing colors.

5. Join the blocks, matching seams.

6. You will need an additional row of sashing and squares at each of the four edges of the quilt top. Lay out 5 sashing strips with 10 small squares for each side of the quilt so that colors alternate with those of the quilt top. Join and add to the quilt, matching seams.

7. Join 4 sashing strips and 10 squares for the top and bottom edges and add to the quilt. Refer to the photo on page 97 for color placement.

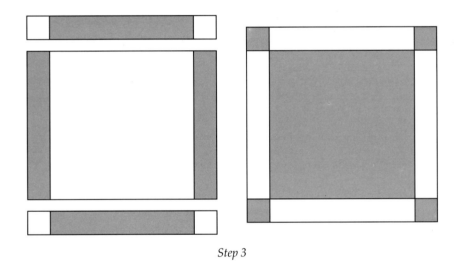

Step 3

ADDING BORDERS

1. Piece the striped border fabrics to get the needed lengths. Add the longer striped borders to the sides of the quilt. Trim so that the ends are even.

2. Add a 2¾" (7 cm) red square to one end of the top striped border. Join to quilt, starting with the red square. Sew to within 8" (20.3 cm) of the opposite end. Measure and trim, allowing ¼" (6 mm) for border seam, and add the second square. Complete the seam, and repeat for the bottom of the quilt.

3. Add the navy border, using the larger red squares in the corners, following the same steps given for the striped border. Press.

BACKING

Join the backing fabrics lengthwise after removing selvages. Press. Trim so that the backing is larger than the quilt top, allowing about 2″ (5.1 cm) extra at all edges. That excess will be trimmed after quilting is completed.

QUILTING

Prepare the backing and batting according to the general quilting directions on page 117. Our quilt is machine quilted using a blue thread in the bobbin with a clear nylon thread on top.

1. Stitch "in the ditch" of all the red and white sashing seamlines, which will give three lines of quilting between the clown blocks. Use continuous lines of quilting the length of the quilt and across the quilt.

2. Stitch in the seamlines of the borders.

3. Last, quilt the clowns. Start at the bottom edge of one shoulder and quilt around each of the heads and hats of these boisterous buffoons.

BINDING

Join the bias binding strips with diagonal seams, matching the stripes to make a continuous strip 8¼ yards (754 cm) long. Add binding according to instructions given on page 120. This binding, bias cut with mitered corners, finishes at ½″ (13 mm).

THE FINAL TOUCH

Now clown it up a little with your signature block. Surround your name with polka dots and stripes or use a posy from a clown's hat. Use three rings to symbolize the circus and to encapsulate the details. You might also add the year in which this performance took place or the town in which it originated. Sew this to the back of your finished quilt, or plan to include it in one of the clown's hats.

ANIMAL FAIR

Here are twenty animals, both wild and domesticated, that we've captured for your quilt. Use the entire menagerie, as we did in our example, or select just a few of your favorites and repeat them.

Make a cat and mouse quilt by repeating and alternating just those two blocks. A farm quilt might include a pig, cow, goat, and sheep, leaving the bear, raccoon, deer, fox, and leopard for a bedcover of wild things. Or use the favorite critter of the child who is going to train these beasts to stay on the bed. All tigers, all frogs, or all lambs in a rainbow array of colors would make charming quilts. There are endless possibilities: the "Gingham Dog and Calico Cat" seems as irresistible as "Baa Baa Black Sheep" or "The Owl and the Pussycat." Santa's reindeer might fill the blocks of a Chirstmas quilt, as long as one bright red nose was included to identify Rudolph.

Each animal face starts with a 5"×6" (12.7 cm × 15.2 cm) rectangle. The corners are trimmed to suggest different species. Half the fun of making this quilt is in finding fabrics that are just right to depict the details. Rummage through all your hoarded scraps with an eye for the texture of an acorn or for the checks that will suggest corn-on-the-cob. The perfect frog green and mouse gray may already be waiting in your remnant box.

It may be helpful to work on just three or four blocks at one time. When those are completed, move on to the next. When two of a particular template are called for, check to see if one needs to be reversed. Just flipping your pattern before cutting will reverse it. Ears, for example, will require flipping to retain a mirror-image while the circular eyes will not.

Read Before Starting Your Quilt on page 15.

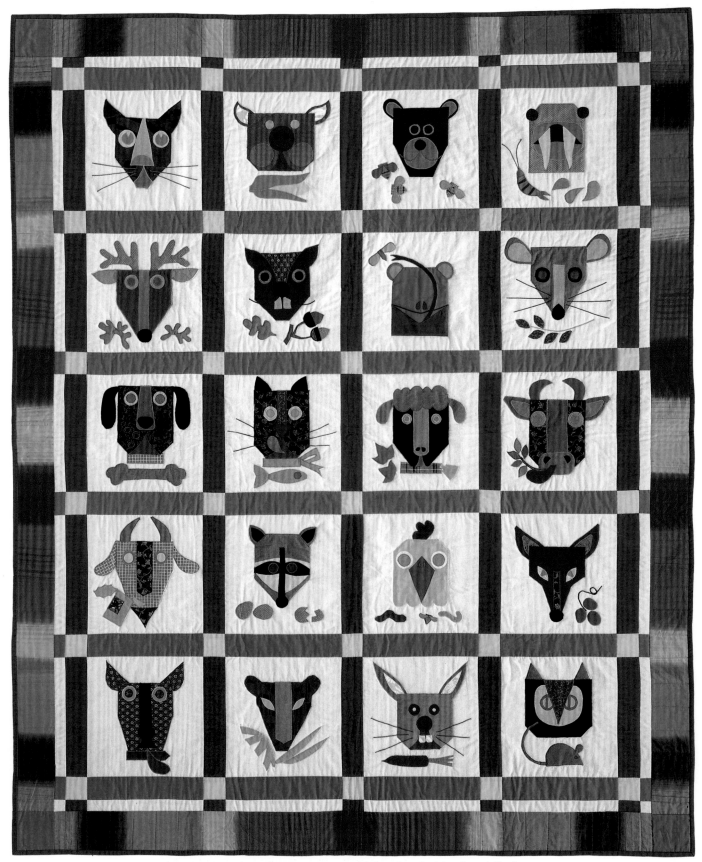

Designed by Jean Ray Laury, assembled and quilted by Susan Smeltzer

Finished size: 62″ × 74½″ (157.5 cm × 189.2 cm)
Finished size of blocks: 10½″ × 10½″ (26.7 cm × 26.7 cm)
Number of blocks: 20
Blocks set: 4 × 5

YARDAGE

Blocks (white): 2 yards (183 cm)
Faces and features (assorted colors and patterns): ¼ yard or less
(23 cm)
Note: Use both solids and prints in an assortment, selecting prints
that suggest appropriate textures.
Sashing, binding (blue): 1⅓ yard (123 cm)
Sashing (green): ⅔ yard (61 cm)
Sashing squares (yellow): ¼ yard (23 cm)
Border (striped): 1 yard (91 cm)
Backing: 4 yards (366 cm)
Batting: 66″ × 79″ (167.6 cm × 200.7 cm)

CUTTING

Blocks (white): 20—11″ × 11″ (27.9 cm × 27.9 cm)
Animal head rectangles (assorted colors): 20—5″ × 6″
(12.7 cm × 15.2 cm)
Sashing
  Vertical (blue): 25—2½″ × 11″ (6.4 cm × 27.9 cm)
  Horizontal (green): 24—2½″ × 11″ (6.4 cm × 27.9 cm)
  Squares (yellow): 60—2½″ × 2½″ (6.4 cm × 6.4 cm)
Narrow sashing
  White: 18—1½″ × 11″ (3.8 cm × 27.9 cm)
  Blue: 10—1½″ × 2½″ (3.8 cm × 6.4 cm)
  Green: 12—1½″ × 2½″ (3.8 cm × 6.4 cm)
  Squares (white): 4—1½″ × 1½″ (3.8 cm × 3.8 cm)
Borders (striped)
  Sides: 2—4″ × 69″ (10.2 cm × 175.3 cm)
  Top and bottom: 2—4″ × 56½″ (10.2 cm × 143.5 cm)
  Squares (green): 4—4″ × 4″ (10.2 cm × 10.2 cm)
Note: Our stripes went from blue and green at one selvage to yellow
at the other. To get a symmetrical effect, we started with the blue
stripes at the corners and moved toward the center. Where the
pieces met, the fabric was seamed. If you use striped material, cut
8—4″ (10.2 cm) strips × width of fabric.

Backing: 2—66″ (167.6 cm) lengths

Batting: 66″ × 79″ (167.6 cm × 200.7 cm)

Binding: 7—2½″ (6.4 cm) strips × width of fabric

ANIMAL FACES

The usual seam allowance is not added to these faces and features, as they are machine appliquéd. Should you prefer to hand appliqué, add ¼″ (6 mm) to each cut edge.

Read the directions for assembling the animal faces before cutting. There are smaller-scale drawings of each face, identified by row. Templates are also provided, and they indicate with broken lines any areas of overlap. Face shapes (next page) and frequently used circles (included with the templates) are numbered. Cut the following:

Row 1-1 Tiger: Face #9 plus 4 pattern parts plus

> **Circles:**
>
> 2 of #11 for eyes
>
> 2 of #8 for eyes
>
> Notch the smaller circles to center, ½″ (13 mm) deep. Remove a small pie-shaped wedge. When appliqué is complete, add lines for whiskers.

Row 1-2 Pig: Face #3 (turn rectangle on its side) plus 6 pattern parts plus

> **Circles:**
>
> 2 of #13 (cheeks)
>
> 1 of #14 (snout)
>
> 2 of #3 (nostrils)
>
> 2 of #5 (eyes)

Row 1-3 Bear: Face #2 plus 5 pattern parts plus

> **Circles:**
>
> 2 of #6 (eyes)
>
> 2 of #3 (eyes)
>
> 1 of #7 (nose)
>
> Add a line for the mouth. French knots can provide the bees with eyes.

Row 1-4 Walrus: Face #4 (turned upside down) plus 9 pattern parts plus

> **Circles:**
>
> 2 of #7 (eyes)
>
> Add lines for the shrimp's antennae.

Row 2-1 Deer: Face #1 plus 5 pattern parts plus

> **Circles:**
>
> 2 of #8 (eyes)
>
> 2 of #4 (eyes)
>
> 1 of #10 (nose)

Animal Faces Diagrams 5" x 6" (12.7 cm x 15.2 cm)

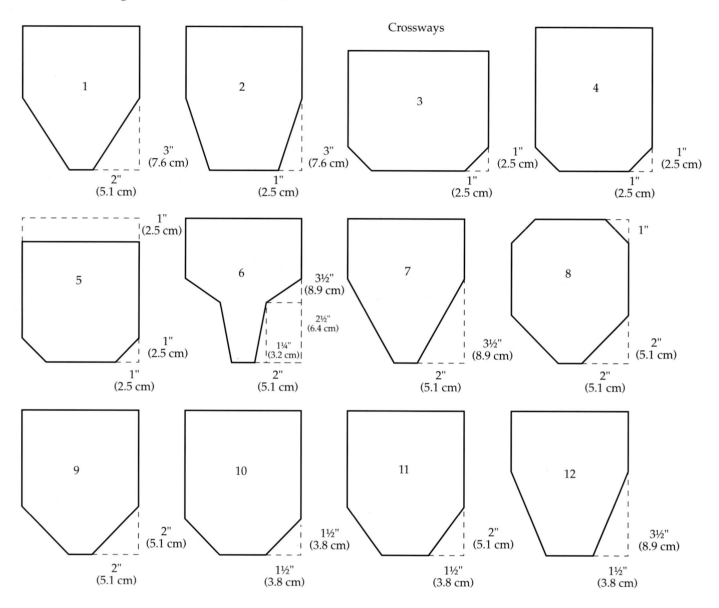

Row 2-2 Squirrel: Face #9 plus 9 pattern parts plus
   Circles:
   2 of #8 (eyes)
   2 of #5 (eyes)
   1 of #10 (nose)
   Freckles were machine satin-stitched, but large French knots or
   polka-dot material would also work. Add line for cheeks.
Row 2-3 Frog: Face #4 (turned upside down) plus 5 pattern
parts plus
   Circles:
   2 of #11 (eyes)
   2 of #8 (eyes)
   Add line for mouth.

Row 2-4 Mouse: Face #7 plus 5 pattern parts plus

> **Circles:**
> 2 of #9 (eyes)
> 2 of #5 (eyes)
> Add lines for the stem and for whiskers.

Row 3-1 Dog with Bone: Face #4 plus 6 pattern parts plus

> **Circles:**
> 2 of #9 (eyes)
> 2 of #6 (eyes)

Row 3-2 Cat: Face #10 plus 9 pattern parts plus

> **Circles:**
> 2 of #8 (eyes)
> 2 of #4 (eyes)
> 1 of #3 (fish eye)
> Add lines for whiskers.

Row 3-3 Lamb: Face #11 plus 9 pattern parts plus

> **Circles:**
> 2 of #6 (eyes)
> 2 of #3 (eyes)

Row 3-4 Cow: Face #5 plus 8 pattern parts plus

> **Circles:**
> 2 of #9 (eyes)
> 2 of #6 (eyes)
> Cut a 2″ × 5″ (5.1 cm × 12.7 cm) rectangle for center of face, and slip it ½″ (13 mm) under nose.

Row 4-1 Goat: Face #12 plus 8 pattern parts plus

> **Circles:**
> 2 of #9 (eyes)
> 2 of #6 (eyes)

Row 4-2 Raccoon: Face #8 plus 6 pattern parts plus

> **Circles:**
> 2 of #6 (eyes)
> 1 of #8 (nose)
> Cut several whole eggs, then cut one apart.

Row 4-3 Chick: Face #4 (turned upside down—mark bottom edge of rectangle at 1¼″ [3.2 cm] intervals, then scallop to suggest feathers) plus 6 pattern parts plus

> **Circles:**
> 2 of #11 (eyes)
> 2 of #8 (eyes)

Row 4-4 Fox: Face #6 plus 6 pattern parts plus

> **Circles:**
> 1 of #9 (nose)
> Add line to make tendril for grapes.

Row 5-1 Dog: Face #2 plus 6 pattern parts plus
   Circles:
   2 of #9 (eyes)
   2 of #5 (eyes)
Row 5-2 Leopard: Face #7 plus 6 pattern parts
Row 5-3 Rabbit: Face #5 plus 6 pattern parts plus
   Circles:
   2 of #7 (eyes)
   1 of #11 (nose)
   2 of #1 (eyes)

   As an alternate to appliquéing the tiny circles in the eyes, find a polka-dot fabric and cut it so that one of the dots suggests the pupil. Add whiskers.

Row 5-4 Owl: Face #3 (turn rectangle on its side) plus 7 pattern parts plus
   Circles:
   2 of #10 (eyes)
   2 of #7 (eyes)
   1 of #1 (mouse eye)

CONSTRUCTING THE BLOCKS

1. Trim the rectangles into faces. Determine what shape is needed and cut according to cutting instructions. Note that several of the faces require that the rectangle be turned on its side before the corners are trimmed.

2. Fold the faces and the background blocks in half and press, making a top-to-bottom crease. Place a face on a background block, aligning the folds to center the head from side to side. Faces move up or down on the blocks depending on the specific animal and its food. Arrange features and any extra details (bone, tin can, and so on) at this time. Tack faces and details in place using a small dab of fabric glue stick. Use the reduced drawings starting on page 111 and the photograph on page 103 as guides for placement.

3. Machine appliqué the animal blocks according to the general directions on page 85. Overlap parts, slipping an edge under an adjacent shape so that both can be appliquéd with one zigzag line. The areas of overlap are indicated on the templates by dotted lines. You will occasionally be appliquéing through several layers at one time. Always start with shapes to be overlapped and larger shapes and work to smaller ones. In sewing the pig, for example, stack all

layers, adhere or pin to secure them, and appliqué the outside (or larger) ear first. The inside ear is next, and the head shape will overlap both. Finally, add nose, then nostrils. With eyes, do larger circles first, then smaller ones.

4. To add detail lines, such as whiskers and stems, sew either by hand or machine as described in Linear Details, page 88. Use the reduced drawing or the photograph as a guide for detail placement.

5. When all animal faces have been sewn and pressed, lay them out to determine their overall placement. Consider the balance of color and of face sizes. It will be helpful to identify the order of the blocks by numbering them so that the arrangement is not lost when you handle them during assembly.

ASSEMBLING THE QUILT TOP

1. Join a blue sashing strip to the left side of each block. Join the blocks in rows of 4 each to give you 5 horizontal rows. Then add a final sashing strip at the right-hand edge of each row.

2. Alternate 5 yellow squares with 4 green sashes to make a strip. Sew this to the top of row 1.

3. Repeat for the tops of rows 2, 3, 4, and 5. On row 5, add an identical strip to the bottom.

4. Join row 1 and row 2. Pin or baste and sew carefully to match seams. Repeat until all rows are connected.

5. For the narrow outside sashing, alternate 5 of the white sashing strips with 6 of the small green pieces. Join to one side of quilt top. Repeat for other side. Make up two similar sashing strips, each with 4 white strips and 5 small blue pieces. Then add a white square at each end. Join one to the top and one to the bottom of the quilt top.

ADDING BORDERS

1. To add final borders, begin by joining the longer borders to the sides of the quilt. Trim. (If you used striped fabric as we did, see the note given in the cutting instructions on page 104.)

2. Add a 4" (10.2 cm) green square to one end of one remaining border. Join border to top edge of quilt, starting with the green square. Sew to within 8" (20.3 cm) of the opposite end. Measure, allowing ¼" (6 mm) for seam on the border, cut, and add the second green square. Finish the seam, and repeat for the bottom edge.

BACKING

1. After cutting away selvages, join the lengths of fabric. This provides a horizontal seamline that runs across the quilt. Trim to fit quilt top allowing 2" (5.1 cm) extra at each edge.

2. Layer the batting and quilt top over the backing as described in the general directions on page 117.

QUILTING

Read the general directions for maching quilting on page 119. Our animals are kept in place through the use of transparent quilting thread on the top, and a blue thread that matches the backing fabric on the back.

1. Sew lines of quilting "in the ditch" on each seamline of the quilt.

2. Each animal face is outlined in stitches sewn as close as possible to the outer edge of the satin stitches. Quilting also outlines all the "extras," such as the animals' favorite foods (ivy leaves, carrots, bones, fish).

3. On the outside border, lines are quilted across the border at 2" (5.1 cm) intervals. When you are quilting in the seamlines of the 2" (5.1 cm) sashings, extend those lines of quilting into the border to the raw edge of the quilt. Those extensions occur all the way around the quilt. That will leave just four short lines of quilting to be added in the spaces between the quilted lines of the sashing extensions. The narrow sashings produce 1" (2.5 cm) quilting spaces at each corner. Refer to the photograph. *Note:* This is the minimum amount of quilting needed to adequately secure the layers of the quilt if you used a bonded batt. You may wish to add a more elaborate pattern.

BINDING

Our blue binding echoes the blue sashing. Join the binding strips with diagonal seams, and add the binding to the quilt top following the directions on page 120 for mitered corners. The binding finishes at ½" (13 mm) wide.

THE FINAL TOUCH

How about cutting one more rectangle to make a "human animal" for the back of your quilt? A portrait of the quiltmaker as animal trainer seems highly appropriate. Date the block and identify the city or barnyard or jungle where you captured these creatures. Perhaps you should name the new trainer and zookeeper as well.

FINISHING

BATTING

Your choice of batting will be determined by several factors: intended use and wear, washability, the spacing of the quilting design, warmth and weight, and appearance. Be sure to read manufacturer's recommendations on the package of batting you purchase. Some batts require quilting at intervals of 2″ (5.1 cm) or less, while others that are bonded or needle-punched require less quilting. Some packages will include washing instructions.

A thinner batt is easier to quilt and allows for much finer quilting. A thicker batt is warmer and softer. Use a thin batt for wall hangings. Use a thick batt for a quilt that will be tied and used on the floor. For a bed quilt, it is a matter of choice.

Although a quilted wall hanging requires less quilting in terms of wear and washability, it makes greater demands for visual effect. A glazed batt makes detailed stitching possible, and the lack of thickness, padding, or warmth is not a disadvantage. Nap pads, used on floors, need padding and thickness.

A quilt that is to be used, washed, dried, and crawled on will benefit from the use of a bonded batt, which survives lots of use and washing. If you intend to tie a quilt or do minimum quilting, use bonded or needle-punch batting.

Both cotton and synthetic batts are available. Each has distinct merits, and it is helpful to handle quilts made from each to determine your own preferences. Cotton remains flexible and does not lose its resiliency. It seems to absorb the stitching, and many quilters prefer it for both hand and machine quilting. It requires close quilting, as the cotton absorbs water during washing and the batting can shift if not held securely in place. Cotton is less likely to "pill" or migrate than a synthetic batt, an important consideration especially if you plan to use dark-colored fabrics.

Because most homes now come equipped with thermostats, the requirements for warmth may be more flexible. If warmth is high on your priority list, use a heavier batting or learn about wool batts.

Synthethic batting washes easily and dries fast. It is lightweight, and (as it does not absorb water) it does not tend to shift during washing. There are various grades of synthetic batting, so look for one that is soft and bouncy rather than wiry and stiff. There should be no lumps or uneven areas in the fibers. Many quilters prefer synthetic batts. We have used both with good results; it is a matter of personal preference. Synthetic fibers seem to have an affinity for one another. Therefore, if you use a synthetic batt and also have some part-synthetic fabrics, you increase the possiblity of "pilling" or migrating.

Batts come in various sizes, and these are stated on the package. Select a batting large enough to fill your quilt in one piece. If you are using by-the-yard batting, you may need to piece lengths together. Butt the cut edges together and whipstitch loosely on both sides.

PREPARATION FOR QUILTING

If you plan to machine quilt, follow these directions for layering the quilt top with batting and backing. At that point, refer to directions for machine quilting. If you plan on tying your quilt, layer according to these directions. Then refer to the *Princess Nap Pad*, Quilting section, for tying instructions.

To use a quilting hoop or to do tabletop quilting (my preferred method) you will need to layer the quilt sandwich and baste carefully. Follow these directions:

Piece quilt backing according to directions given for the individual quilt. Press backing and finished quilt top. Place quilt backing fabric face down on a large smooth area (a table or the floor). Tape the backing to a wood surface, or pin to a tight-pile carpet, so that the backing is held taut and smooth. Place batting loosely on top of the backing. Place the quilt top face up on batting, allowing an excess of 2″ (5.1 cm) backing and batting at all edges. Pin at the edges. Baste the three layers together, using a long sharp needle (darning needle) and a long strand of cotton thread. Start at the center and work outward on large quilts. On quilts of about 48″ (121.9 cm) wide or less, baste all the way across in one direction. Baste every 3″ to 4″ (7.6 cm to 10.2 cm) in both directions, and add diagonal lines, corner to corner.

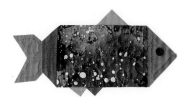

Trim the batting, allowing enough to fill the binding plus ½″ (13 mm). Trim the backing, allowing several inches extra. Fold the backing over the batting and baste to the edge of the quilt top. This will keep the batting out of the way and prevent fraying.

The layers can now be quilted on a table top. This same process is used if you intend to quilt with a quilting hoop. If you intend to quilt on a frame, follow the manufacturer's instructions for the best method of attaching the layers and preparing the quilt.

If you are brand new to quilting and feel the need for additional help, check with a local quilt shop, a quilt guild, other quilters, or your library for good references. There are many good books on quilting, including *Quilts! Quilts!! Quilts!!!* by McClun and Nownes.

QUILTING

Your quilt top can be transformed into a quilt by any of several methods: hand quilting, machine quilting, or tying. Always use the best quality thread you can obtain.

HAND QUILTING

If quilting thread is not available in the color you need, substitute sewing thread rubbed lightly with beeswax. You can use a shorter, thin-shafted quilting needle (number 9, 10, or 11 Between). My preference is for a longer, thin-shafted needle (Sharp) for tabletop quilting.

Use a single thread about 25" (63.5 cm) long, knotted on the end. To conceal the knot, put the eye end of the needle into the backing fabric where you wish to start the first stitch. The eye will go between threads rather than splitting a thread as the point can do. The opening can be stretched slightly by moving the needle eye back and forth. When you make your first stitch, give a slight tug to pull the knot into the hole. Use your fingernail to scrape over and close up the hole. A tiny backstitch secures the thread.

The consistency of your stitch length is most important. Keeping the length constant is more essential to a satisfying appearance than the number of stitches to the inch. To maintain small stitches front and back, the length of each stitch must occur between stitches and will be buried in the batting. Angle the needle slightly between stitches, rather than stitching straight up and down. See diagram 1.

Quilt long lines first, to secure the layers together. When quilting the blocks, sew in long straight lines, letting the stitches of a second line cross those of the first line at the corners. Avoid turning the corners with the quilting stitches themselves as that tends to round them out, losing the geometric design. Diagrams showing quilting patterns make this clear. It will be necessary to turn corners with quilting when appliquéd pieced images are to be outlined.

In tabletop quilting, keep both hands on top of the quilt. Assuming you are right-handed, use the fingers of the left hand to spread the fabric slightly, keeping it taut between the index and middle finger.

Diagram 1

Stitch in that space, letting the needle just touch the tabletop before bringing it back up. With a little practice you can make fine quilting stitches on both back and front in this way. This method keeps the quilting very portable.

A quilting hoop provides another way of adding a little tension to the layers while stitching. Follow the instructions that come with the hoop. Or better still, watch a quilting friend demonstrate the process.

MACHINE QUILTING

Baste the layers together firmly for machine quilting. Or safety pins can substitute for basting. Use 1" (2.5 cm) rustproof pins, placing them 3" to 4" (7.6 cm to 10.2 cm) apart over the entire top. Place them between your quilting lines so that they will not have to be moved as you sew.

Use a size 80 or 90 needle and regular sewing thread. You are less likely to encounter problems if you use all-cotton thread both on top and in the bobbin. If you prefer clear or smoky nylon, use it only on top. Because of its transparency, it does tend to disappear into the seams.

For long straight lines (sashings, borders) and for outlining, use the walking foot on your machine, and allow the machine to move the fabric. Roll the sides of the quilt to make the bulk of the material easier to handle.

To set up for freehand quilting, first consult your sewing machine manual. Freehand work allows you to stitch in any direction without turning the whole quilt. The needle slides over the pattern as if you were using a pencil to draw the design. (Except that the "pencil" is stationary and you move the "paper" around beneath it!) Following the print of a fabric can be a very effective way of doing freehand quilting. The background of *Goosie Goosie Gander* is done in this way. Or you can do a meandering stitch, keeping the pattern random and crossing over previous stitching as little as possible.

Generally, the directions for freehand quilting are as follows:
1. Drop the feed dogs (on some machines, they get covered with a special plate).
2. Remove the utility foot and replace with a darning foot. (See your sewing machine dealer for one that fits your particular machine.)
3. Loosen the tension of the top thread slightly so that only the top thread is visible on the quilted line. Use about the same setting as when you sew a buttonhole satin stitch.
4. Place quilt under the needle and drop the needle into the fabric, taking one stitch. Raise the needle and pull bobbin thread through to the top. Hold both threads as you start sewing. Backstitch to

secure ends, and then guide the fabric to create the design under your needle. Do not turn the quilt, but let it glide or float under the needle.

5. Even out the speed of the machine with the movement of your hands to get consistently even stitches. (It's like patting your head while rubbing your tummy—not too easy the first time.)

6. Backstitch to secure thread ends, and clip ends close to fabric. Clipping the thread ends as you go makes the finishing faster and less tedious.

7. Relax. It gets to be fun. If you make what you consider an error, it can easily be removed. When you are free forming the design over a patterned material, it is hard to identify a "mistake."

TYING

Tied quilts are often referred to as comforters, and they tend to be thick and fluffy. The thick batts are difficult to quilt, thus the preference for tying. One of the quilts in this book, a nap pad, is tied. Refer to the *Princess Nap Pad* for specific directions on tying. The process will be similar for any other quilt you wish to tie.

BINDING

Binding is the final step in making a quilt, unless you have not yet signed it. It not only finishes the edge, but is also an important part of the overall quilt design.

The color chosen is usually one used elsewhere in the quilt. A dominant color from the quilt top is a likely choice, either the darkest or the brightest. The strong color used helps to contain or frame the quilt. When making a decision about the binding color, it is helpful to pin your quilt top on a wall so that you can try strips of several different values and colors. You will know when you have found the right one, as the combination will be satisfying and the repetition of color will make the quilt look complete.

Use either bias- or straight-cut bindings. If you prefer squared corners, work with the measurements given with each quilt. If you prefer mitered corners, join the lengths to make a continuous binding. When using bias binding, care must be taken to avoid stretching the fabric, so the binding will lie smooth and straight. The bindings themselves are pieced with diagonal seams, pressed open, as in diagram 2. The extra fabric required for corners has already been figured into the measurements.

If you wish to add a sleeve, so that your quilt can be hung, sew it onto the quilt with the binding. Read the section on Adding Sleeves, page 122, before sewing bindings.

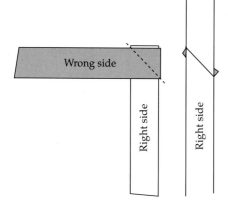

Diagram 2

A double binding method simplifies the final hand sewing and gives added strength to the edge. All the quilts in this book, with the exception of the *Princess Nap Pad*, were finished with double binding. This measurement is determined by multiplying the desired finished width by four and adding the two seam allowances. For example, a ½″ (13 mm) binding requires a strip 2½″ (6.4 cm) wide.

Before adding any binding, baste the outside edges of the quilted top.

SQUARED CORNERS

Fold the cut binding in half lengthwise with right sides of the fabric out. Press. Place the binding on a side edge of the quilt with the cut edges of the binding aligned with the cut edge of the quilt top. Let the binding extend 1″ (2.5 cm) past each end of the quilt. Pin or baste the binding in place, checking to be sure the layers are aligned. Stitch on the seamline from one end of the quilt to the other. Repeat for the other side. The stitching will go through both layers of the binding and all layers of the quilt.

Trim batting and backing on the two sewn edges, measuring from the binding seamline. Batting should extend to the width of the finished binding. For example, with a ½″ (13 mm) binding, cut your batting to ½″ (13 mm) or just slightly wider, but be careful not to cut it any smaller. If batting does not fill the binding completely, there may be loose or concave areas that will give the binding an uneven appearance.

Trim the ends of the bindings so that cut edges are flush with the ends of the quilt. Fold the binding to the back of the quilt and slip stitch the folded edge to the seamline on the quilt back, making sure that the binding is well filled. If any area looks as if the binding will collapse, or look empty, add wisps of extra batting to fill it.

Add bindings to the quilt top and bottom according to diagram 3, allowing excess binding fabric at each end. Sew top binding seam over the finished side binding. Fold the binding to the back and, starting several inches from one corner, slip stitch it to the seamline as shown in diagram 4. At the corners, fold the end of the bindings to the back; see diagram 5. Trim as necessary and slip stitch in place. Then fold the width of the binding over to meet the seamline as in diagram 6. Trim any excess batting, seam allowance, or backing to avoid a bulky corner. Slip stitch in place. This will give a neat square corner to the quilt. Finish remaining corners.

CONTINUOUS BINDING

A continuous binding must be equal in length to the perimeter of the quilt, plus a few inches. Fold the binding in half lengthwise with right sides out and press. Starting on a side of the quilt (not at a corner),

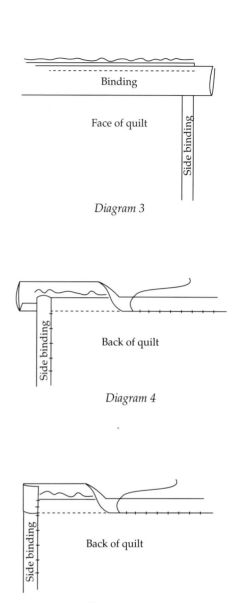

Diagram 3

Diagram 4

Diagram 5

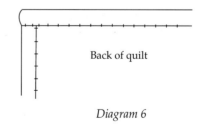

Diagram 6

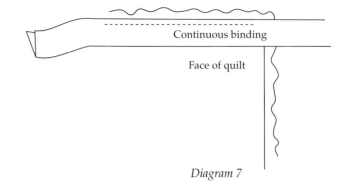

Continuous binding

Face of quilt

Diagram 7

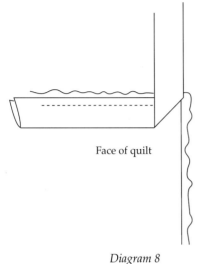

Face of quilt

Diagram 8

Face of quilt

Diagram 9

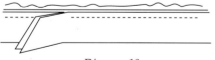

Diagram 10

pin the binding to the quilt, raw edges together. Using a ¼″ (6 mm) seam, sew to within ¼″ (6 mm) of the corner (diagram 7). Backstitch and cut thread. Remove quilt from the machine and fold the binding strip at a 90-degree angle, away from the quilt, as shown in diagram 8. Then fold the binding straight down, ready to cover the next side (diagram 9). When turned, that will create a perfect mitered corner. Check the first corner to make sure it is accurate. If not, fold a little more or a little less fabric as needed to make a perfect miter. Complete all corners. Where the ends of the bindings meet, trim each, allowing 1″ (2.5 cm) of overlap. Fold the top binding under and complete the seam (diagram 10), catching both beginning and ending binding in the seam. Fold the binding to the back and whipstitch the folded edge to the seamline.

ADDING SLEEVES

If you wish to hang a quilt, it will be important to add a sleeve or channel through which a rod or pole can be inserted. That will provide a means of hanging and will support the weight of the quilt. Add the sleeve at the top edge of the quilt. A 3″ to 4″ (7.6 cm to 10.2 cm) (finished size) sleeve is standard, so you will need to double that width and add a seam allowance. For a 3″ (7.6 cm) sleeve you will need a 7″ (17.8 cm) width. The finished length should be about 1″ (2.5 cm) less than the width of the quilt.

A secure sleeve or channel can be sewn to the quilt before the binding has been finished. That way, channel and binding can be added with a single seam. Cut the sleeve from cotton fabric and hem the short ends. Fold the sleeve in half lengthwise with the right sides out. Place the cut edges of the sleeve on the top back of the quilt so that raw edges are aligned with raw edges of the quilt. Place the binding on the front of the quilt (the opposite side) and stitch binding and sleeve to the quilt with one seamline. After the binding is turned and hand stitched to the top seamline, slip stitch the bottom folded edge of the sleeve to the quilt back, being careful not to sew through to the front of the quilt.

This will hold the sleeve down and hide it when the quilt is hung. Slip a pole or rod through the sleeve to hang the quilt.

SIGNING

Somewhere near the completion of the quilt it is important to sign it. That must certainly be done before the quilt leaves your hands. And if the signature is to be incorporated into the design of the quilt it must be planned early on. Include any or all of the following: who it's for; who the quilter is and her relationship (aunt, mother, neighbor); where, why, and when it was made.

Consider a thread or floss color that is compatible with the quilt. It should have a contrast similar to other colors of the quilt. For instance, if you have made a quilt in pastels, don't sign it in black or your signature will overpower everything. But if there is no contrast (a black thread on navy fabric), it'll be lost completely. Choose one of the contrasts that already appears in the quilt.

If you are writing a youngster's name as well as the quilter's, you may prefer to use big block letters, which are easily read by a child. If the recipient is past fifteen (or past forty) the lettering can be smaller and more intricate.

The inclusion of more detailed information always adds interest to a label. The occasion (birthday? graduation?) for which the quilt was made may be pertinent. Any other personal or family information that interests you should be added.

Suggestions about where to put your signature have been given all the way through the book. Here are some suggestions on how to make a label.

- Using an extra fine line permanent marker (Sanford's Sharpie® for example), write your name, date, and town on a piece of cloth or onto a pieced block. Appliqué this to the back of the quilt.
- Follow a traditional example and quilt your name right into the quilt. Sometimes just initials are quilted. The use of initials for a first name with the last name written out is common, but it's a good idea to include a maiden name to clarify family identification. You don't want someone thirty years from now assuming your sister-in-law (who thinks quilters just a trifle odd) made your quilt.
- Embroider your name onto a border or into the sashing. The lower right-hand corner is the time-honored spot for this signature. You can write your name in longhand or block letters using a sharp silver or white pencil. Then stitch exactly over the line using outline stitch or running stitch.
- Run a piece of fabric into your typewriter and type your name and all pertinent information on a piece of cotton fabric. Heat set. The

permanence is affected by both the ribbon and the fiber content of your fabric, so test for washability (just dip it in a little soapy water, rinse, and iron on the back side).

• Write your name with one of the new sewing machines that does everything, including your correspondence.

• Use a photo transfer method to add a picture of the quiltmaker and lucky kid to the label. Add names and dates.

• Use a rubber stamp set with permanent (India) ink in the stamp pad. Stamp the information onto a separate piece of fabric. Use 100 percent cotton for best results, and print the black ink on any color that relates to the quilt. Practice on scraps until you get a feel for the right amount of ink needed on the fabric. Sew the fabric to the back of the quilt. *Note:* Should you ever wish to display or exhibit your quilt, identify it carefully on the back. If you have added a sleeve to the quilt, slip a piece of cardboard into it while you write, using a permanent marker, on the sleeve. Give your name, phone number, dimensions, and so on in large, clear letters. Any directions about hanging can also be included. This precludes any loss or misplacement of your work due to torn or lost paper labels.

CARING FOR YOUR QUILT

Kids' quilts get constant use. They *will*, in all probability, be washed, so fabric selection is important. Look for washability and color-fastness. Test for color fading or running and prewash all material. Read the manufacturer's label for washing instructions.

A preferred method of cleaning quilts is by hand washing (in a bathtub) and drying them face down on the grass. But not everyone has the time, the energy, or the grass. Therefore, consider durability when you make your choices of batting, quilting pattern, and fabric.

Some mothers, enthusiastic in their efforts to create a relatively germ-free environment, toss quilts into the washer with alarming frequency. Continuous machine washings will wear out any fabric! Quilts can often be shaken or aired to restore freshness. Hand spot-washing of a soiled area may be all that is needed. Wash the quilts only when it is necessary.

Although we can help prolong the life of a quilt, it will eventually fade or wear with constant use and frequent washings. The eventual softening of colors adds a new quality. And because fading seems inevitable, perhaps it should (like freckles or gray hair) be viewed philosophically and accepted with grace. Many treasured quilts are faded and worn, mute evidence of their histories. But they are still around, and that tells us they were loved.

LESSON PLAN

Quilt Shop Guidelines: 5 sessions, 2½ hours each.

SUPPLY LIST

Scissors, for paper and fabric	Interfacing
Needles, sewing and quilting	Quilt fabric
Sewing machine	Backing
Thread, sewing and quilting	Batting
Pins	Pin-up board for demonstration
Small remnants of Ultra Suede® or other nonwoven fabric (optional)	

Note: Students should not make final fabric decisions until a sample block has been made up.

SESSION 1

1. Give each student a pattern for Fish 1.
2. Have each cut a fish from patterned fabric and a background from solid.
3. Without sewing them, place the parts together and use the mock-up as a guide in choosing fabrics. Using a pin-up board, try each fish on a variety of backgrounds. Discuss the contrast of value and color and see which combinations seem most satisfactory.
4. Help each student determine colors. Suggestions to students could include making all blocks in dark values, in polka dots, in a single color, or in color families (blues and greens, violets and magentas). Bright, light fish on darker background blocks create the most graphic effects. For a more complex and subtle effect, try patterned backgrounds and plain fish, alternated with the reverse.
5. Repeat process with Fish 2.

6. Cut sashing strips in assorted colors (do 8 or 10 ahead of time) and place them between the background blocks. Use the pin-up board so that all students can easily see the effects of varying contrasts. Help students determine sashing colors.

7. Encourage students to bring remnants of a great variety of prints for the fish and fins, and encourage them to trade. These fabrics will be supplemented with those they need to buy.

8. Analyze which fish work best in terms of the scale of the fabric patterns. Suggest other variations: use all striped fish, only large-scale prints, or all solids. Search for patterns that resemble fish scales or waves. Encourage individual ideas so that each quilt will be unique.

9. By the end of the session, students should know the color range in which they wish to work.

10. Homework: Collect, gather, or purchase the fabrics needed to make at least the first 6 to 8 blocks.

SESSION II

1. Using the patterns, cut out one Fish 1 and one Fish 2.
2. Demonstrate how to sew the curved line on Fish 1. Assemble.
3. Demonstrate how to make the prairie points for Fish 2.
4. Assist students as they assemble the 2 fish.
5. Demonstrate the use and sewing of nonwoven fabric for eyes.
6. Demonstrate how to face an assembled fish and turn it, being sure to include the prairie points on Fish 2. Demonstrate careful pressing so that no facing peeks through; demonstrate basting if necessary.
7. Show students how to fold and center the finished fish on the background.
8. Demonstrate the appliqué stitch to secure the fish to the background fabric.
9. Homework: Complete up to 10 blocks. Bring them finished and pressed.

SESSION III

1. Have class members share their most successful block combinations.
2. Pin up finished blocks and check the sashing color selected. When satisfied, cut all sashing pieces.
3. Work on remaining fish, reversing the directions of some.
4. Demonstrate assembly of blocks with sashing, giving particular attention to the alignment of seams.
5. Homework: Finish all blocks; add sashings to complete top.

SESSION IV

1. Pin a finished quilt top up on the wall.
2. Have pre-cut fabric strips ready to try for border colors. Suggest the inclusion of colors used within the quilts.
3. Make color choices and cut all borders.
4. Demonstrate how to add borders, giving special attention to corners.
5. Discuss the backing and batting; determine batting size needed.
6. Discuss the selection of backing fabric: what's appropriate, amount of fabric needed, how to piece it.
7. Demonstrate stacking and preparation of the quilt layers for quilting, and discuss various quilting methods.
8. Homework: Complete the quilt top, stack and baste in preparation for quilting.

SESSION V

1. Demonstrate the marking or measuring for ¼" (6 mm) lines.
2. Demonstrate techniques of hand quilting. Include making concealed knots as well as hiding the end of the quilting thread.
3. Distribute diagrams of quilting patterns to be used on the fish, such as scales, diamonds, diagonals, stripes. For those who quilt on a tabletop or with hoops, quilting can be started in the classroom. Those who prefer a quilting frame will have to do this at home.
4. Demonstrate sewing the folded binding, with emphasis on square corners.
5. Make sure students have received the help they need and feel ready to proceed on their own.
6. Remind students to sign and date their finished quilts. Show examples.
7. Set up a future date for the students to return with finished quilts. If possible, plan a small exhibit in the shop or a time for sharing and showing.

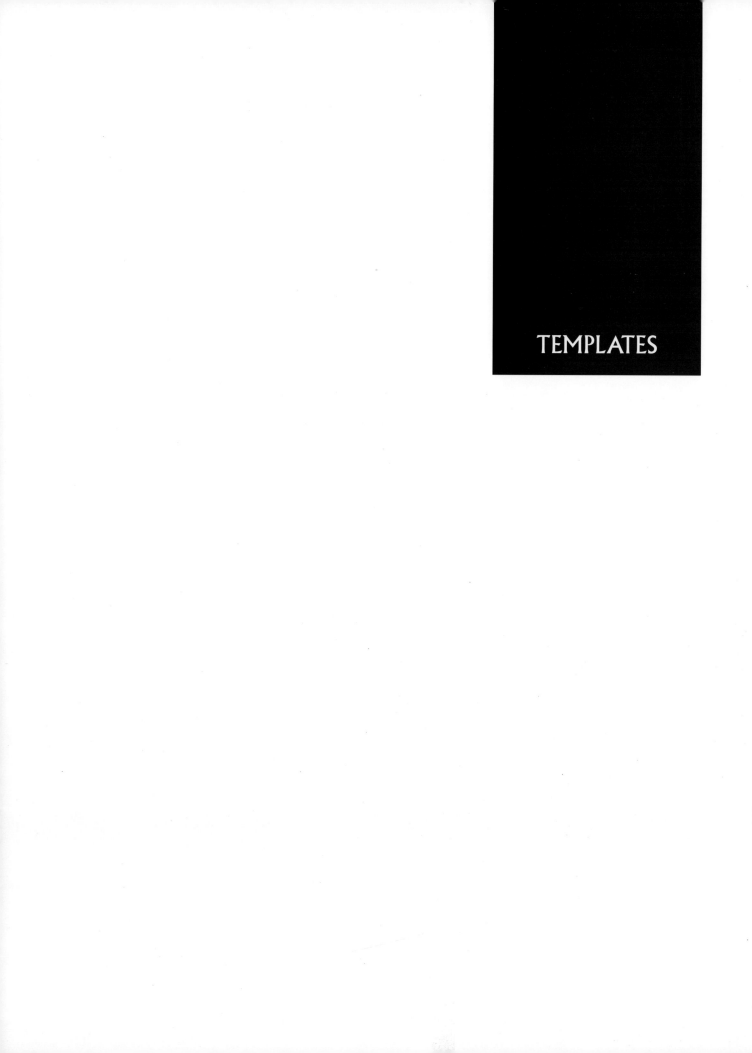

TEMPLATES

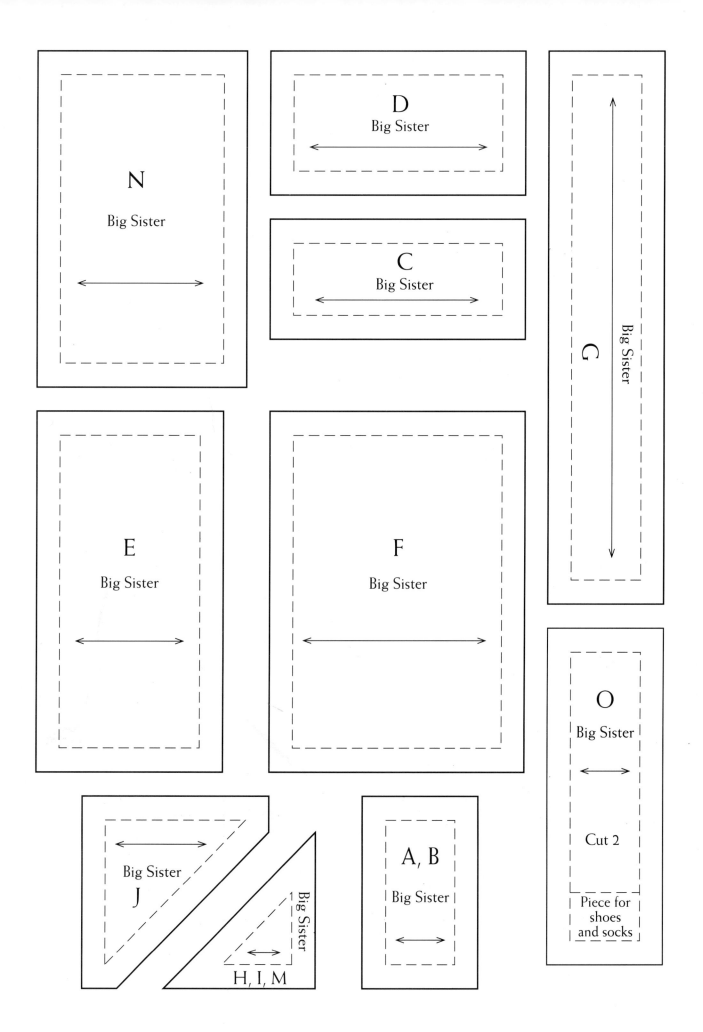

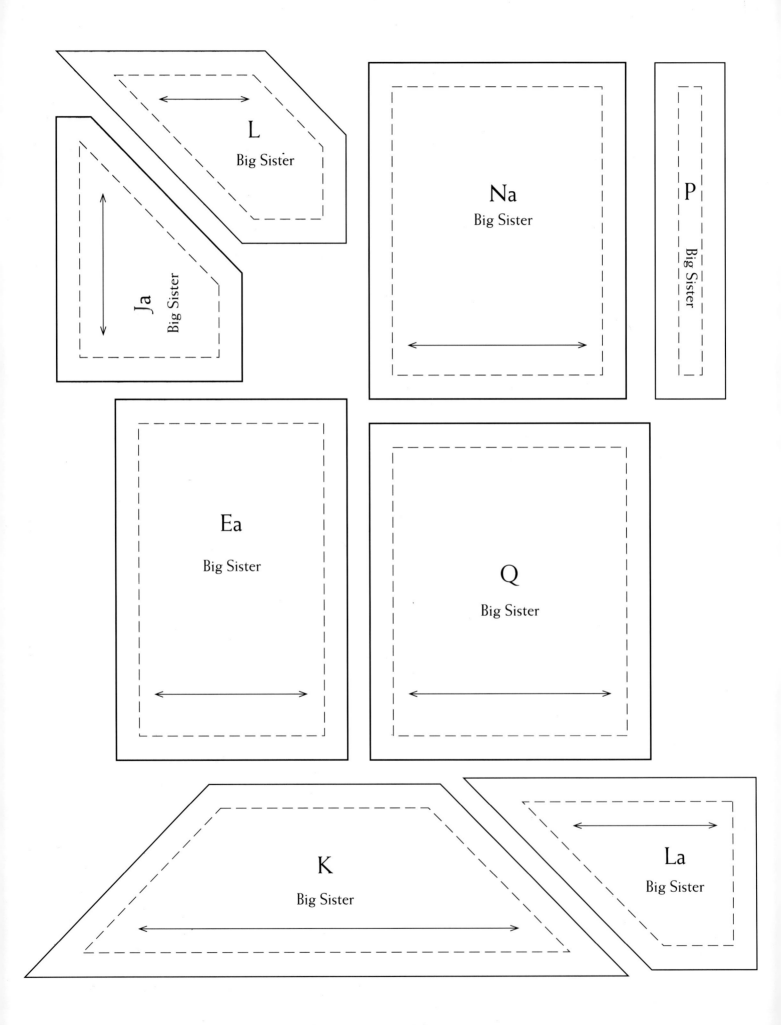

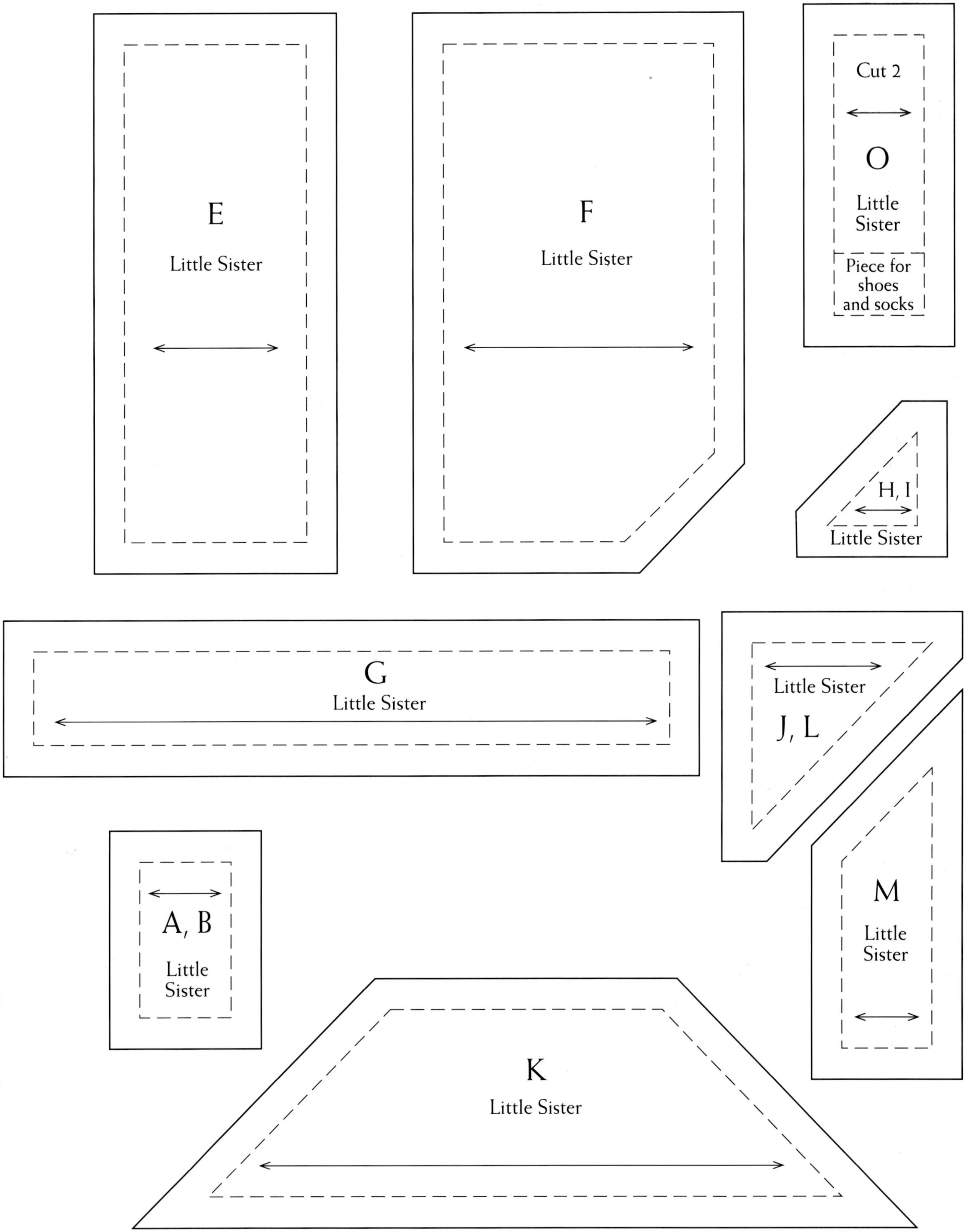

E

Little Sister

F

Little Sister

Cut 2

O

Little Sister

Piece for
shoes
and socks

H, I

Little Sister

G
Little Sister

Little Sister

J, L

M

Little Sister

A, B

Little
Sister

K

Little Sister

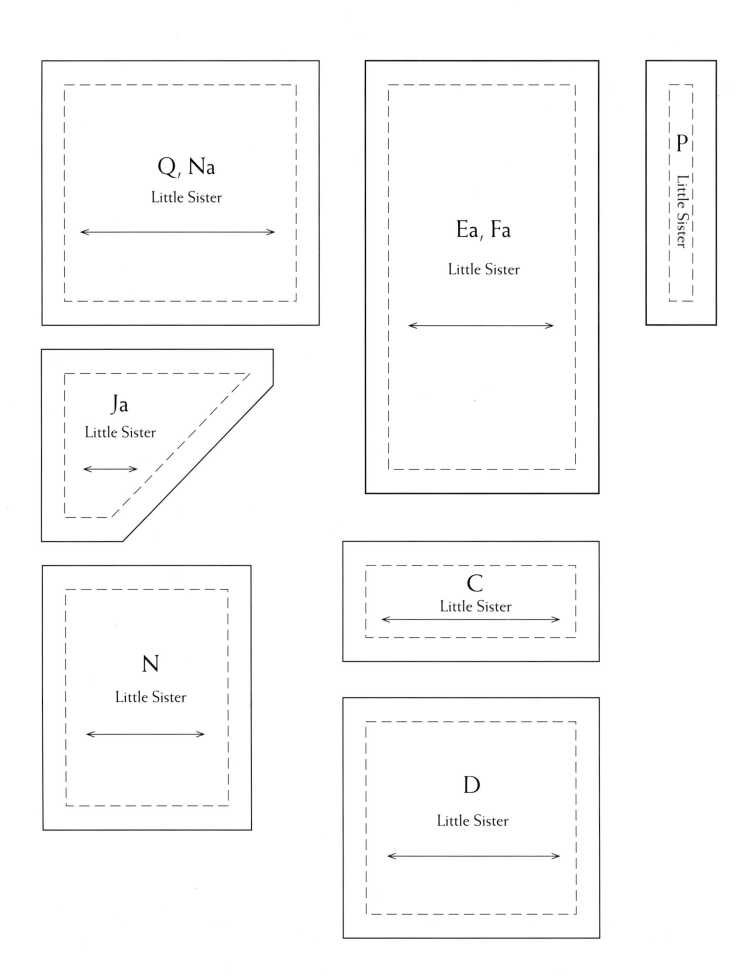

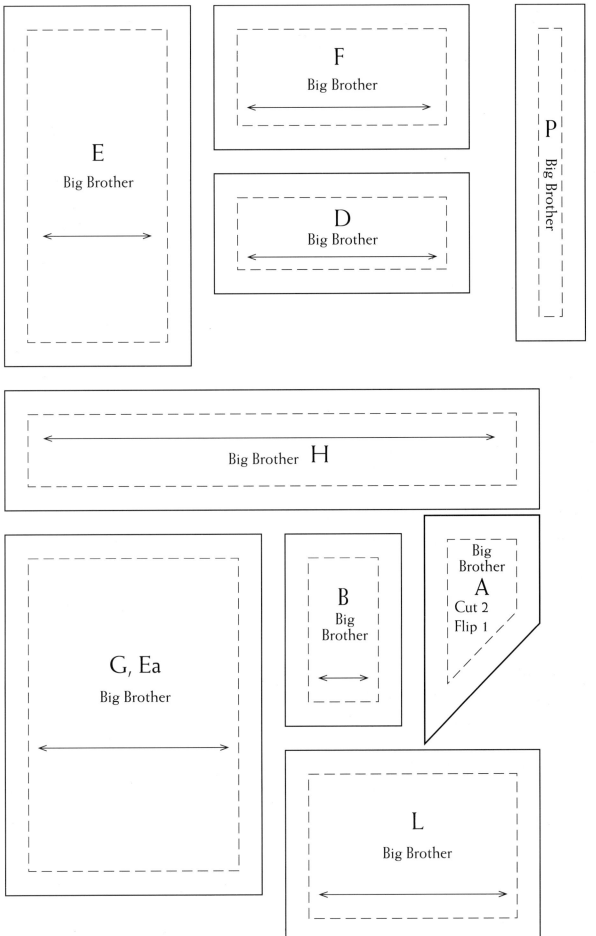

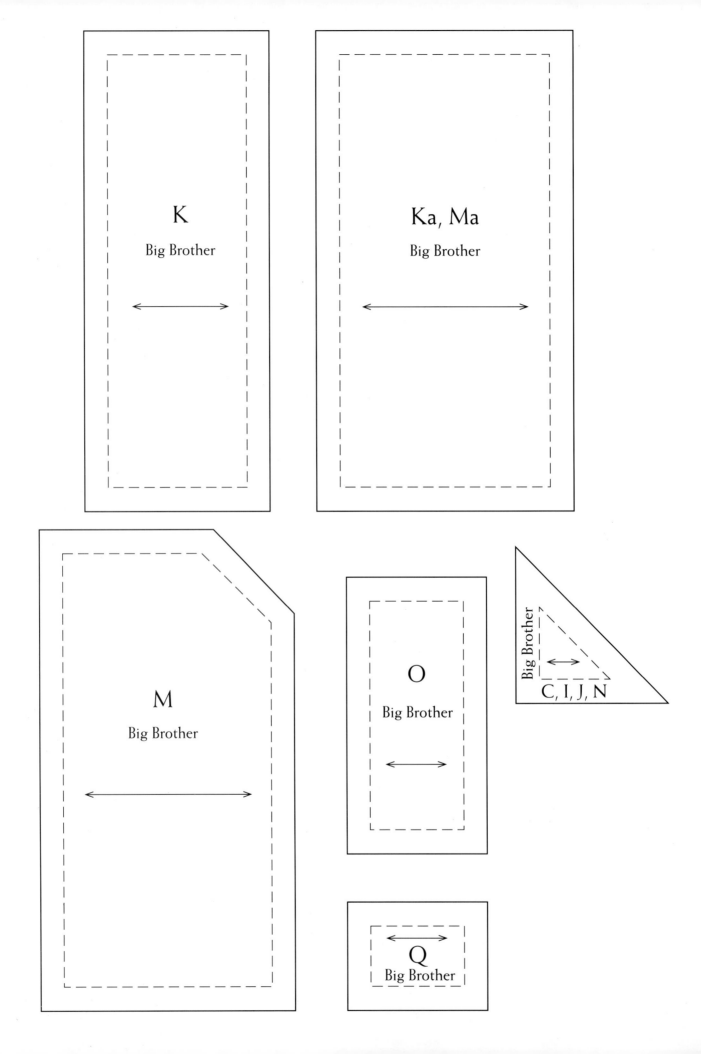

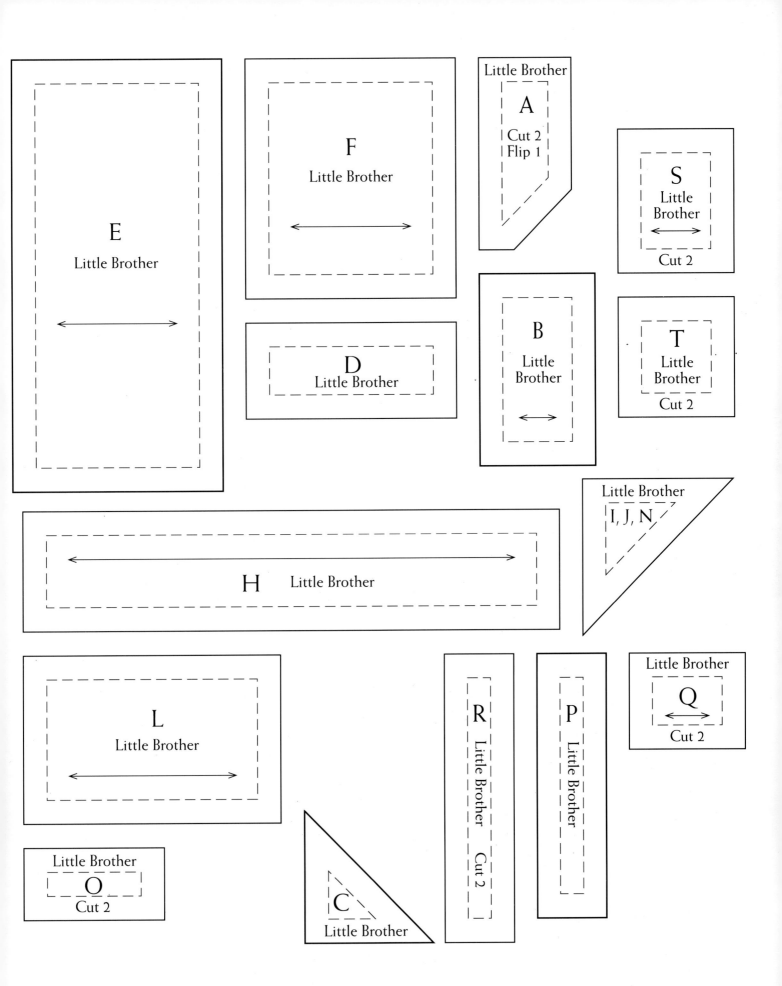

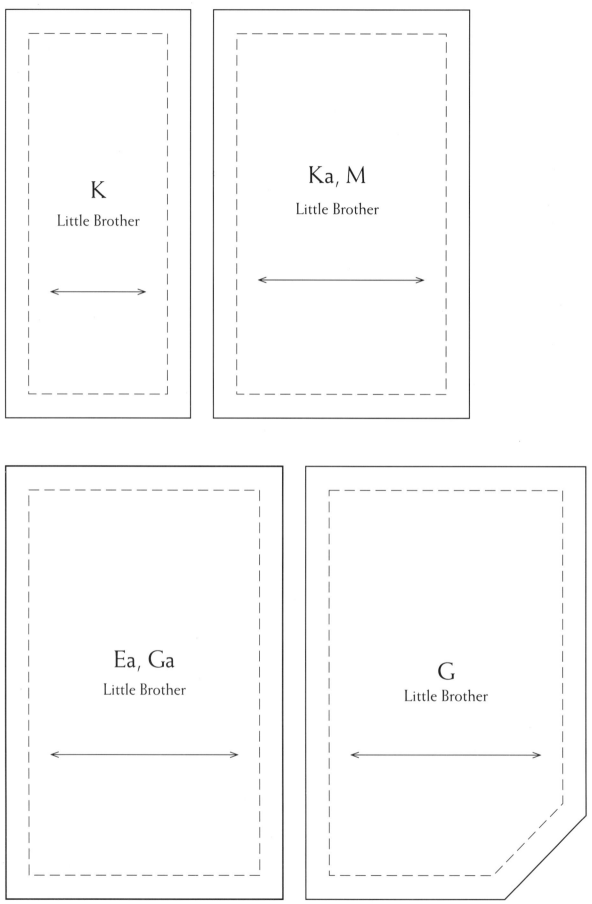

K

Little Brother

Ka, M

Little Brother

Ea, Ga

Little Brother

G

Little Brother

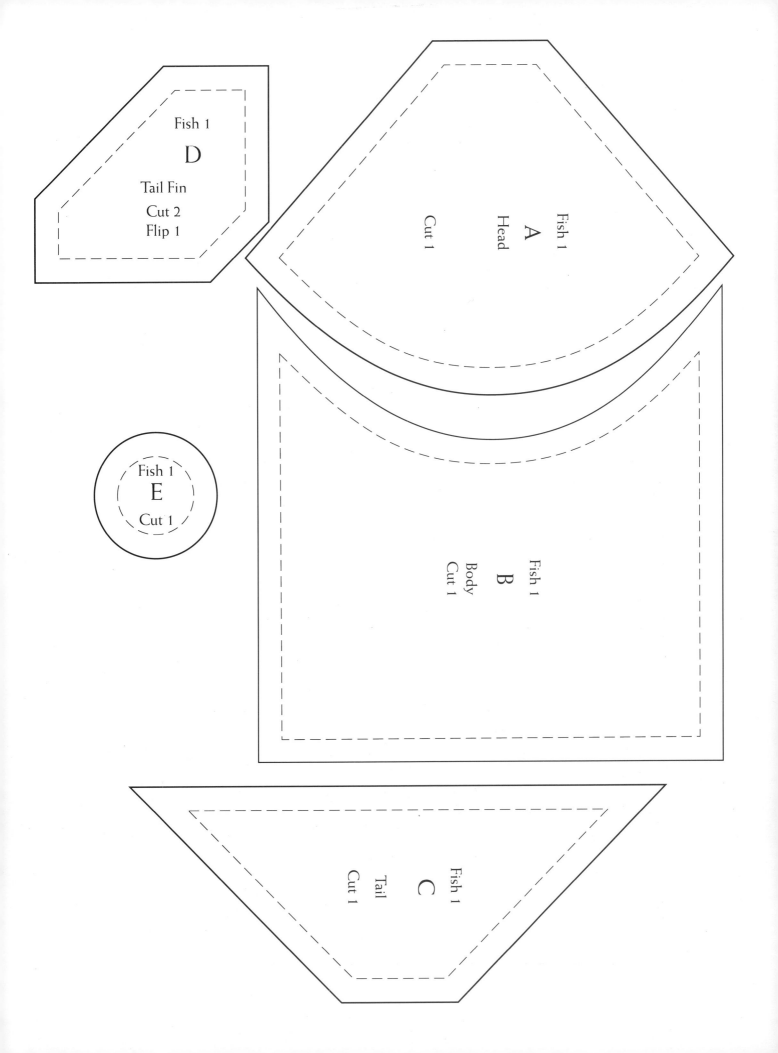

Fish 1

D

Tail Fin

Cut 2
Flip 1

Fish 1

A

Head

Cut 1

Fish 1

E

Cut 1

Fish 1

B

Body
Cut 1

Fish 1

C

Tail

Cut 1

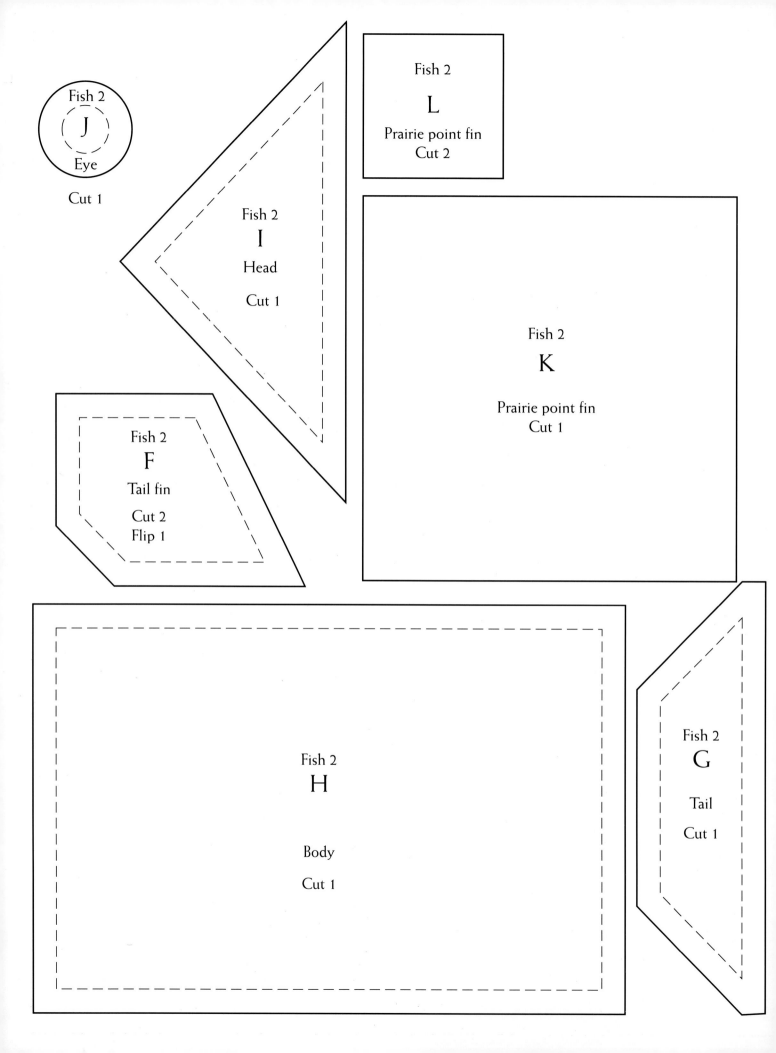

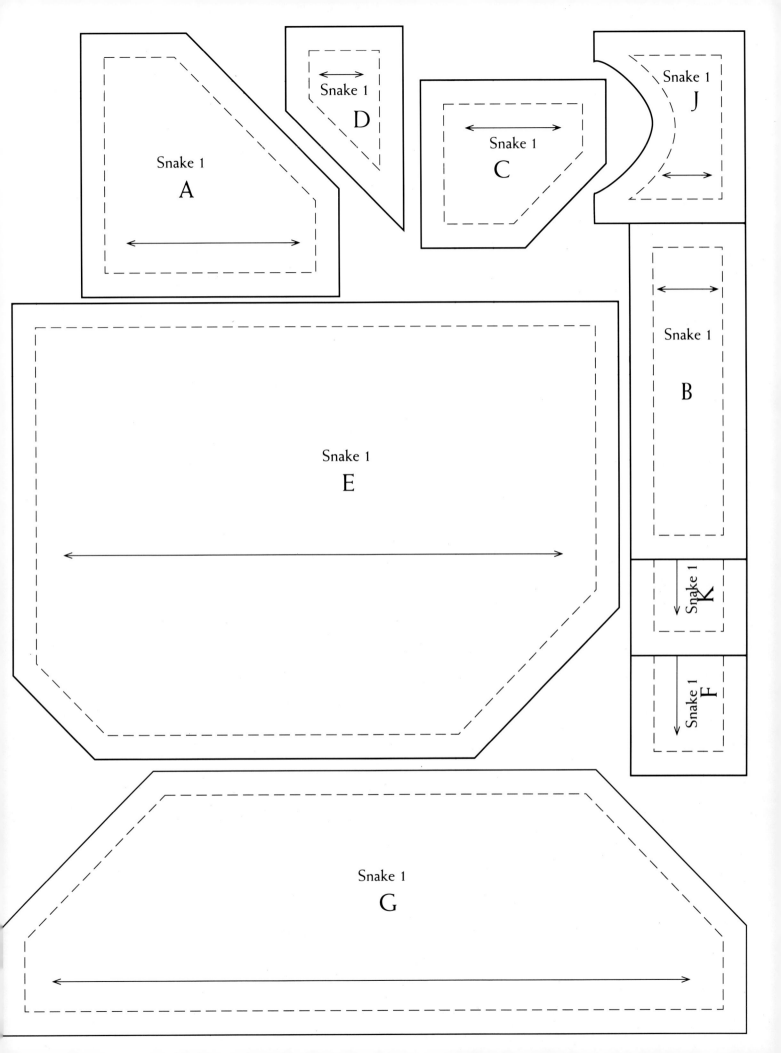

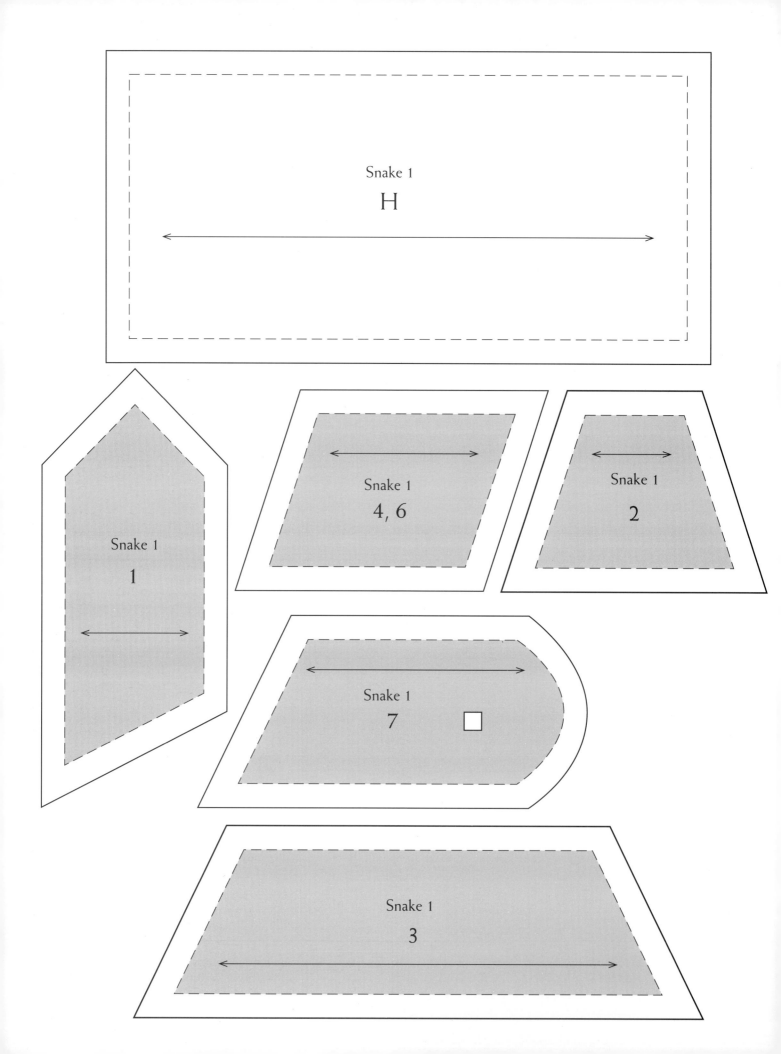

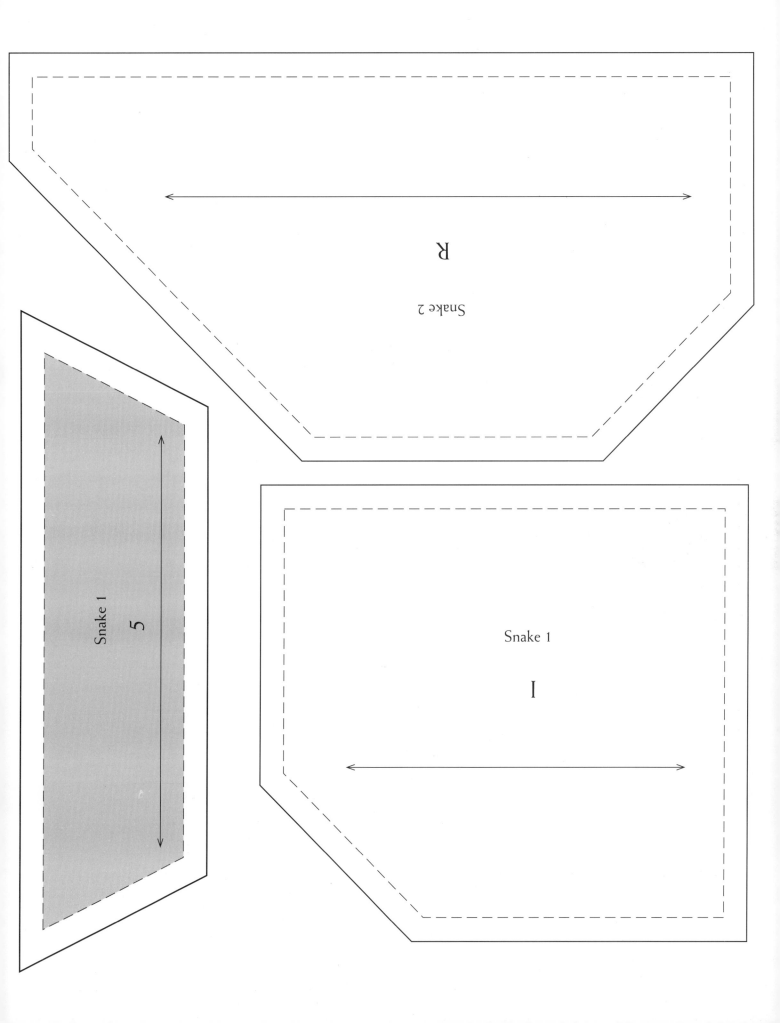

Snake 2

Я

Snake 1

I

Snake 1

5

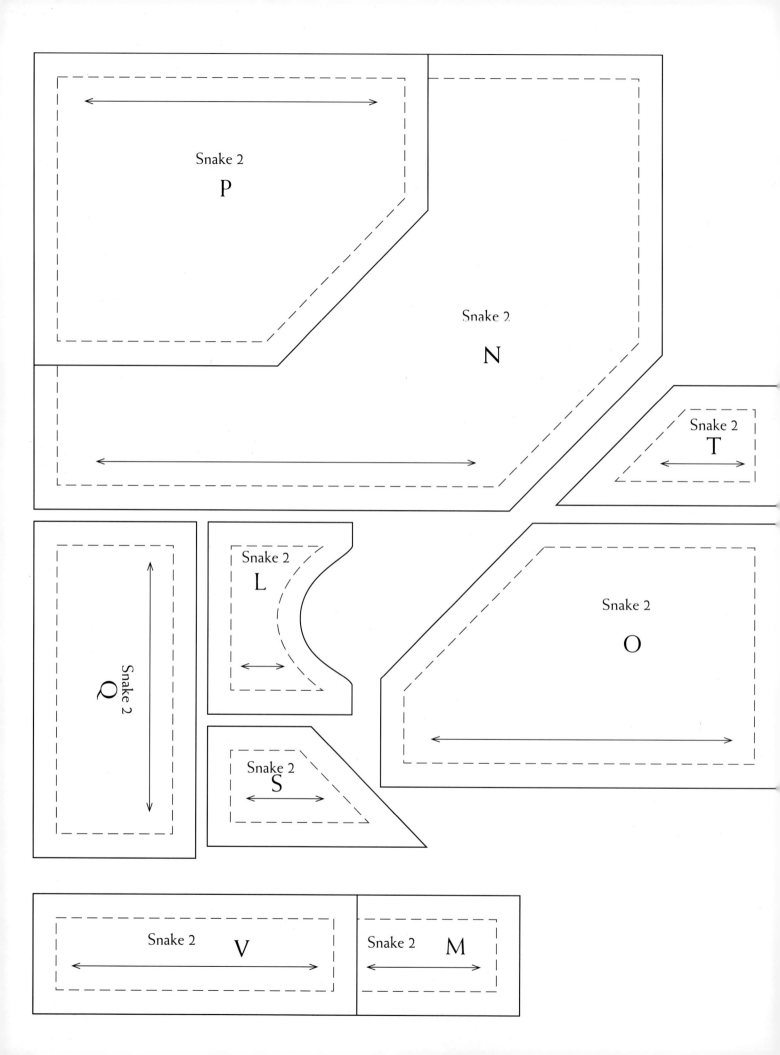

Snake 2
P

Snake 2
N

Snake 2
T

Snake 2
L

Snake 2
O

Snake 2
Q

Snake 2
S

Snake 2   V

Snake 2   M

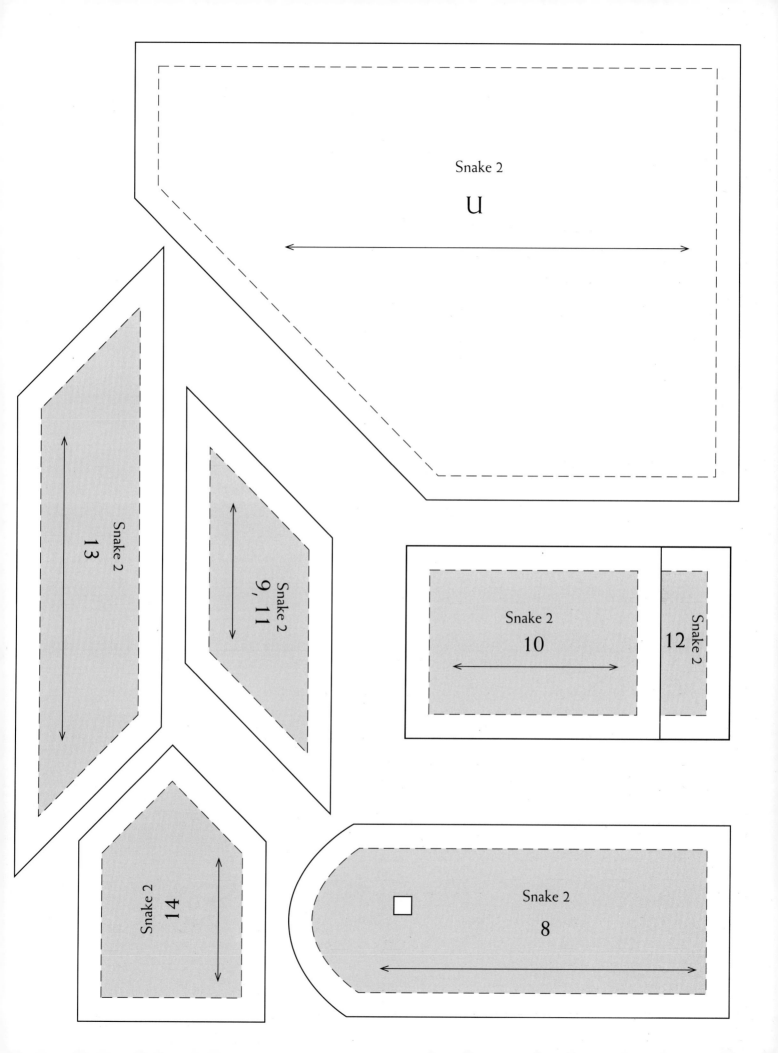

Snake 2

U

Snake 2

13

Snake 2

9, 11

Snake 2

10

Snake 2

12

Snake 2

14

Snake 2

8

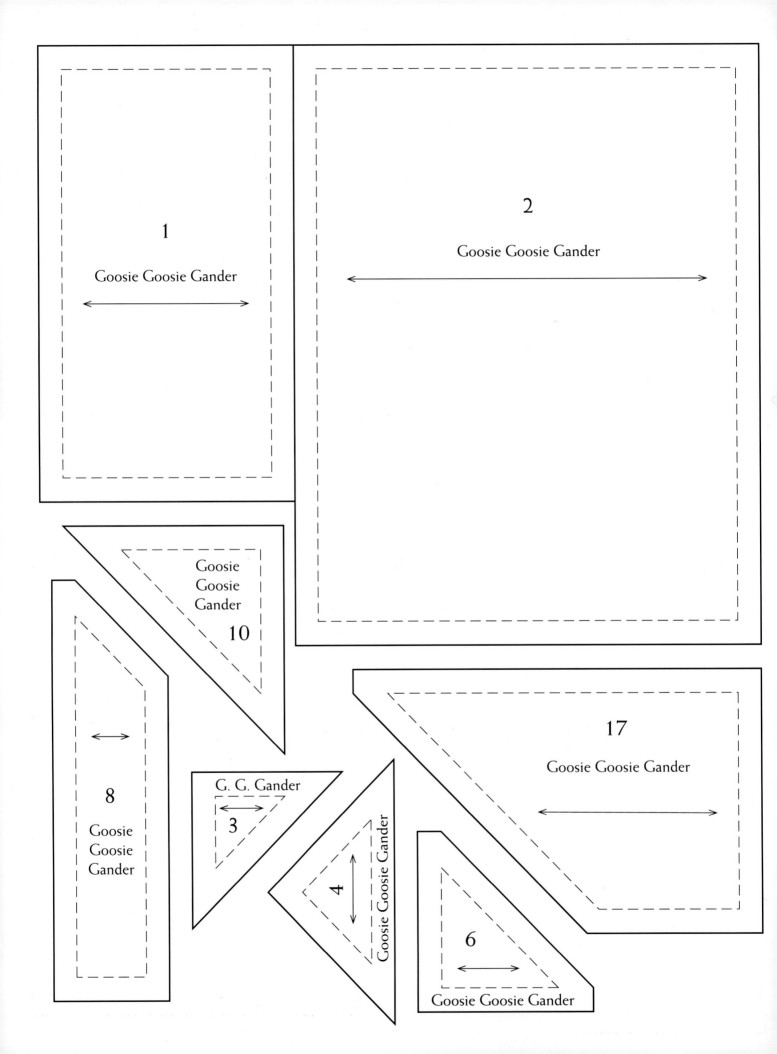

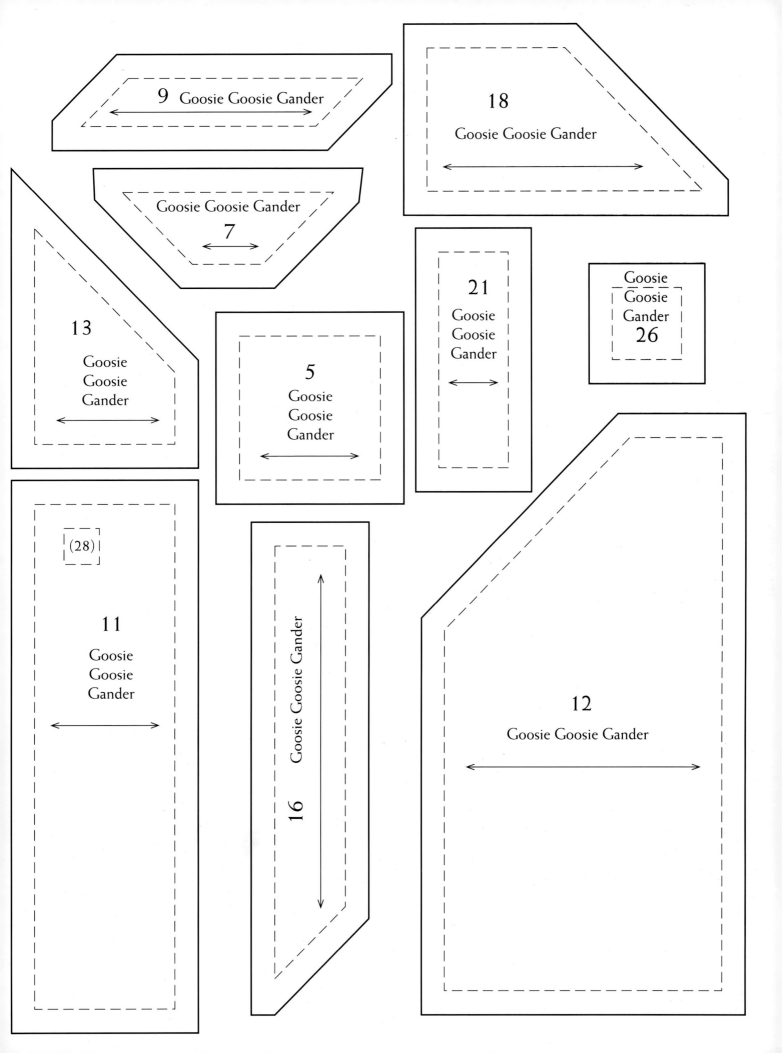

9 Goosie Goosie Gander

18 Goosie Goosie Gander

Goosie Goosie Gander
7

13 Goosie Goosie Gander

5 Goosie Goosie Gander

21 Goosie Goosie Gander

Goosie Goosie Gander 26

(28)

11 Goosie Goosie Gander

16 Goosie Goosie Gander

12 Goosie Goosie Gander

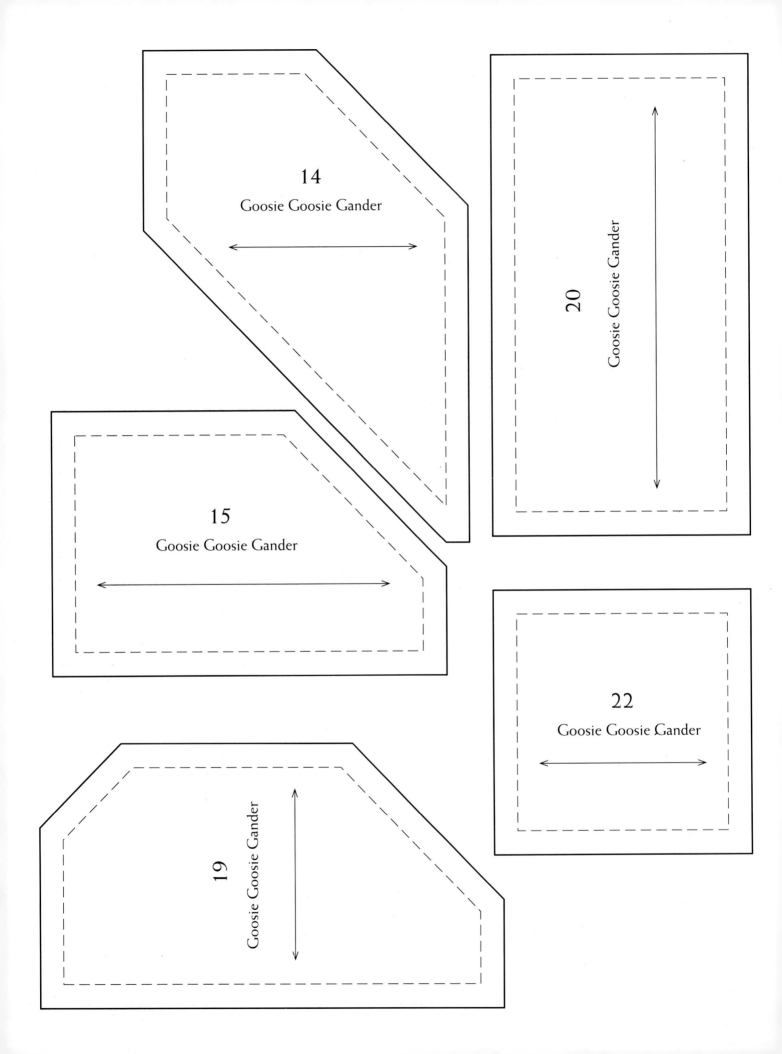

14
Goosie Goosie Gander

20
Goosie Goosie Gander

15
Goosie Goosie Gander

22
Goosie Goosie Gander

19
Goosie Goosie Gander

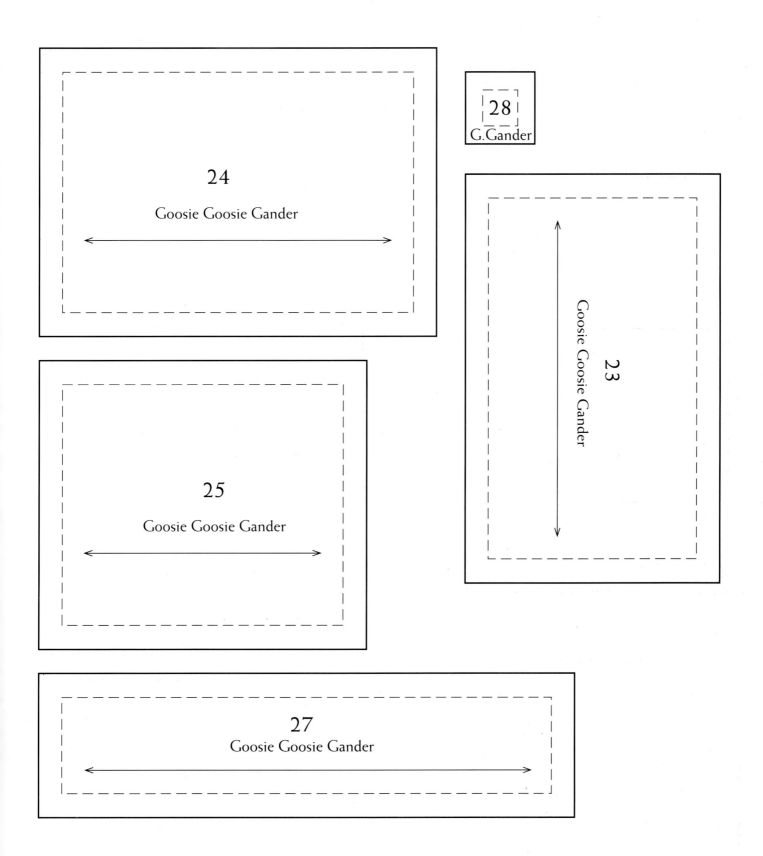

24

Goosie Goosie Gander

28

G.Gander

23

Goosie Goosie Gander

25

Goosie Goosie Gander

27

Goosie Goosie Gander

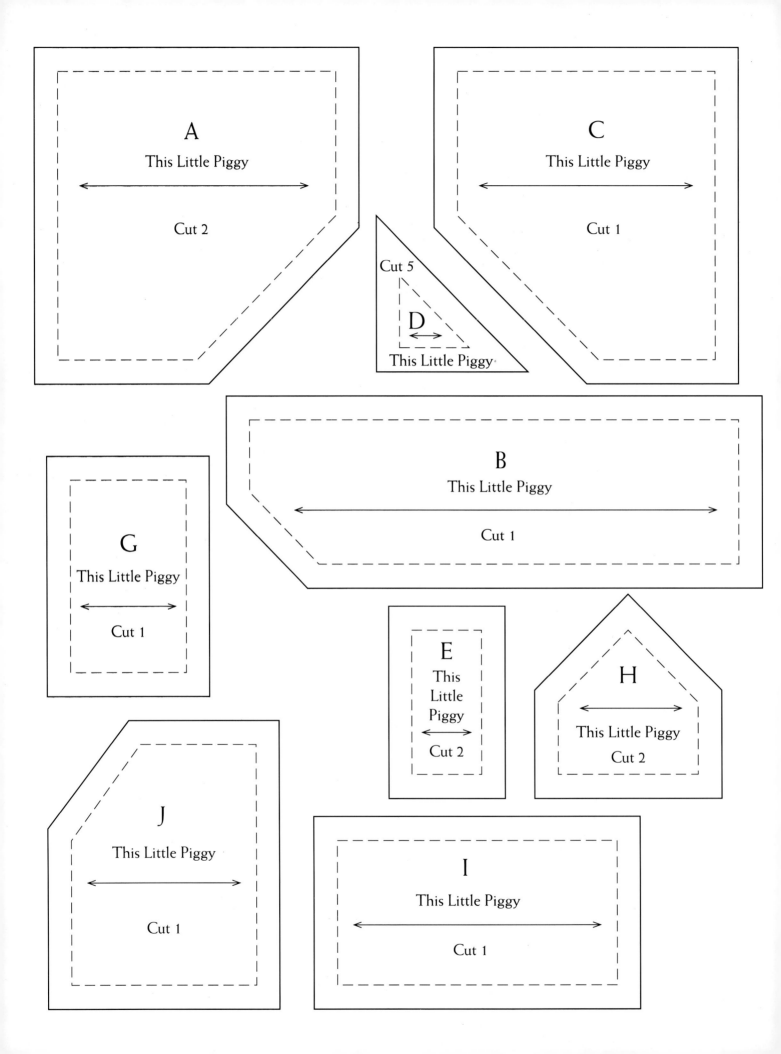

A
This Little Piggy
Cut 2

C
This Little Piggy
Cut 1

Cut 5
D
This Little Piggy

B
This Little Piggy
Cut 1

G
This Little Piggy
Cut 1

E
This
Little
Piggy
Cut 2

H
This Little Piggy
Cut 2

J
This Little Piggy
Cut 1

I
This Little Piggy
Cut 1

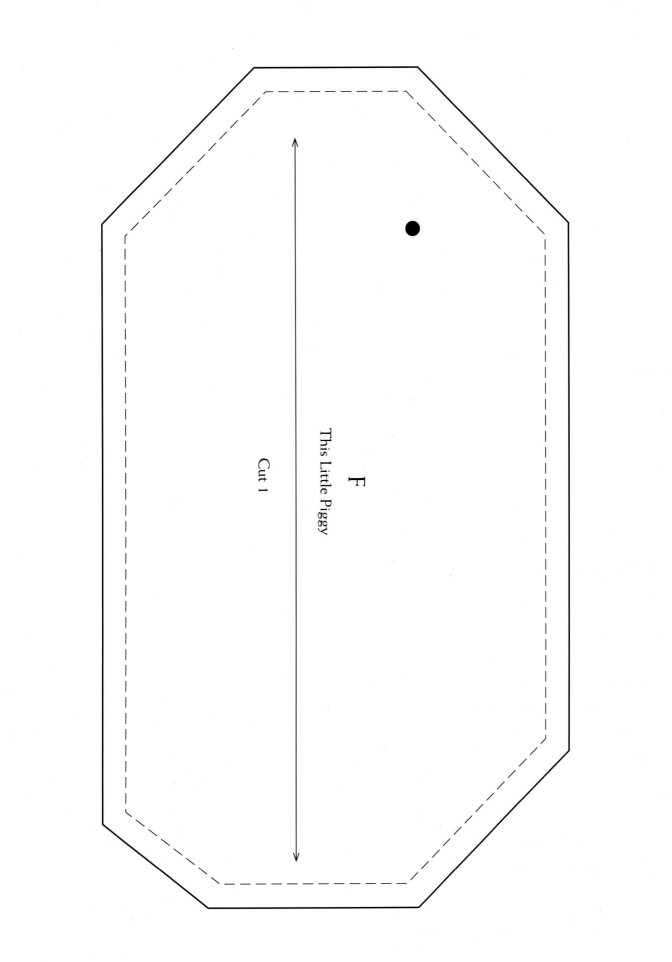

F

This Little Piggy

Cut 1

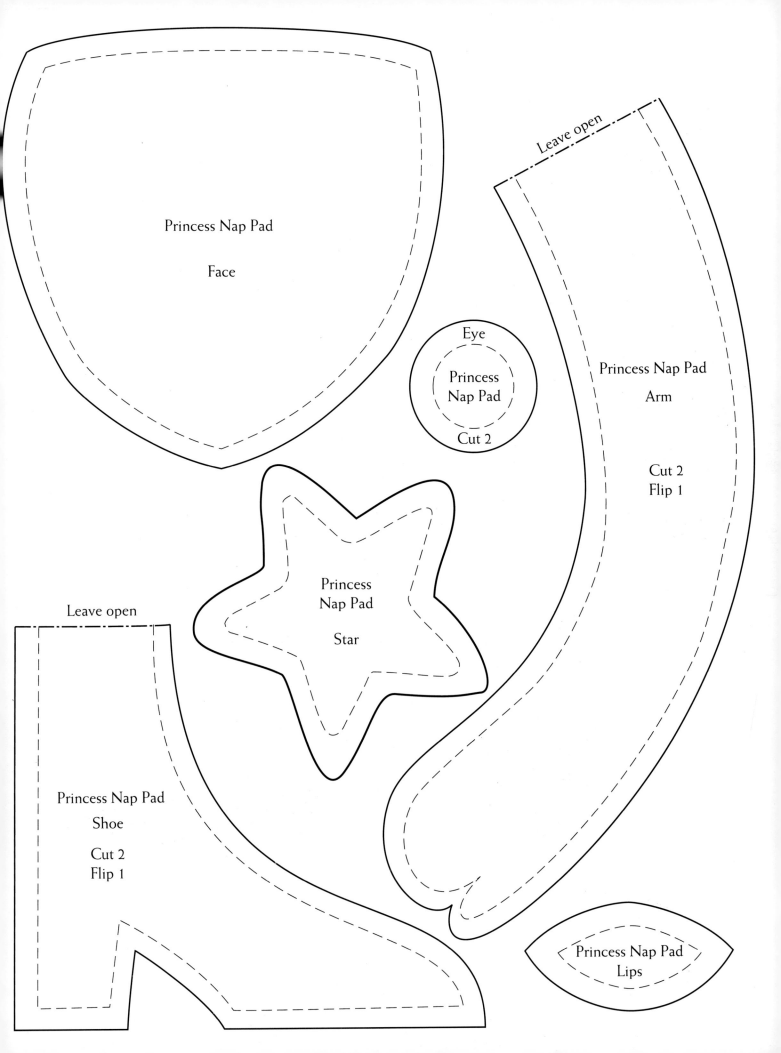

Princess Nap Pad

Face

Leave open

Princess Nap Pad

Arm

Cut 2
Flip 1

Eye

Princess
Nap Pad

Cut 2

Princess
Nap Pad

Star

Leave open

Princess Nap Pad

Shoe

Cut 2
Flip 1

Princess Nap Pad
Lips

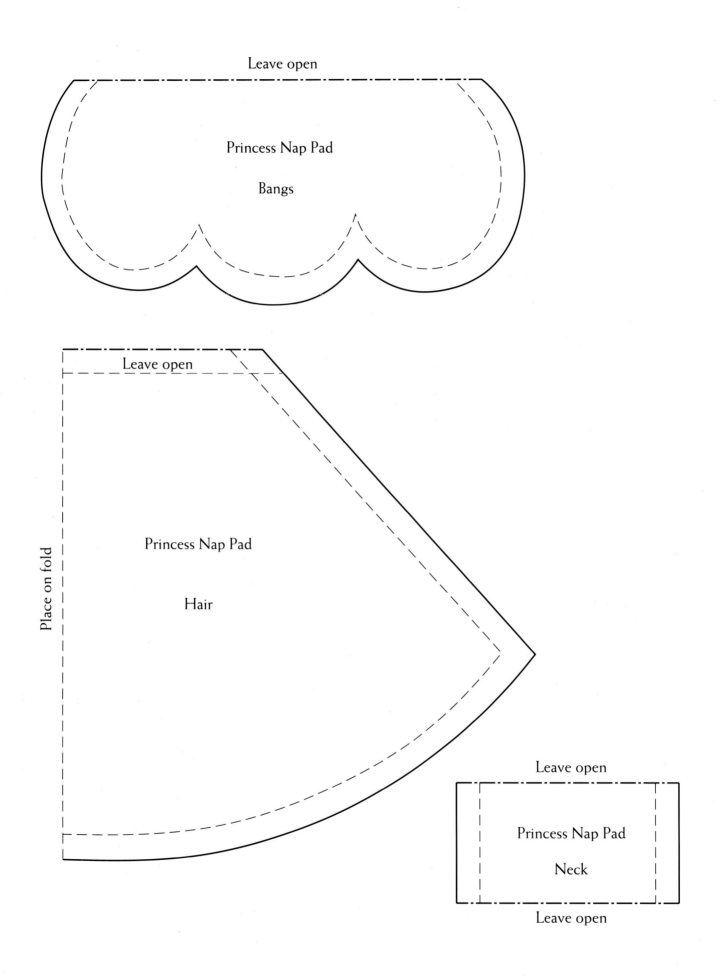

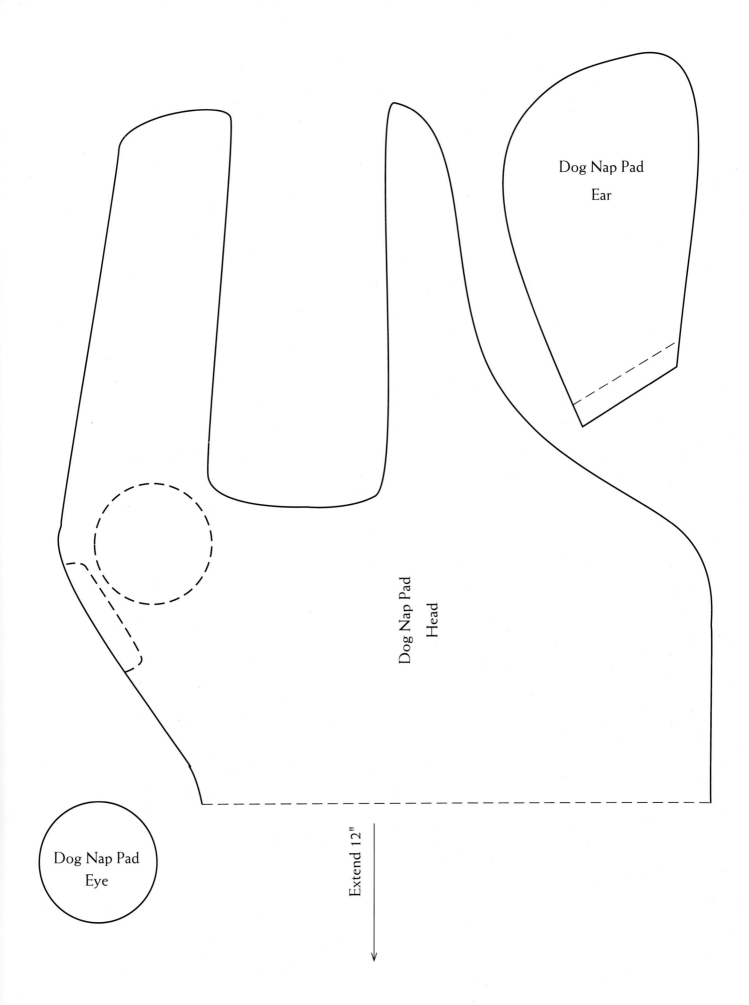

Dog Nap Pad
Ear

Dog Nap Pad
Head

Dog Nap Pad
Eye

Extend 12"

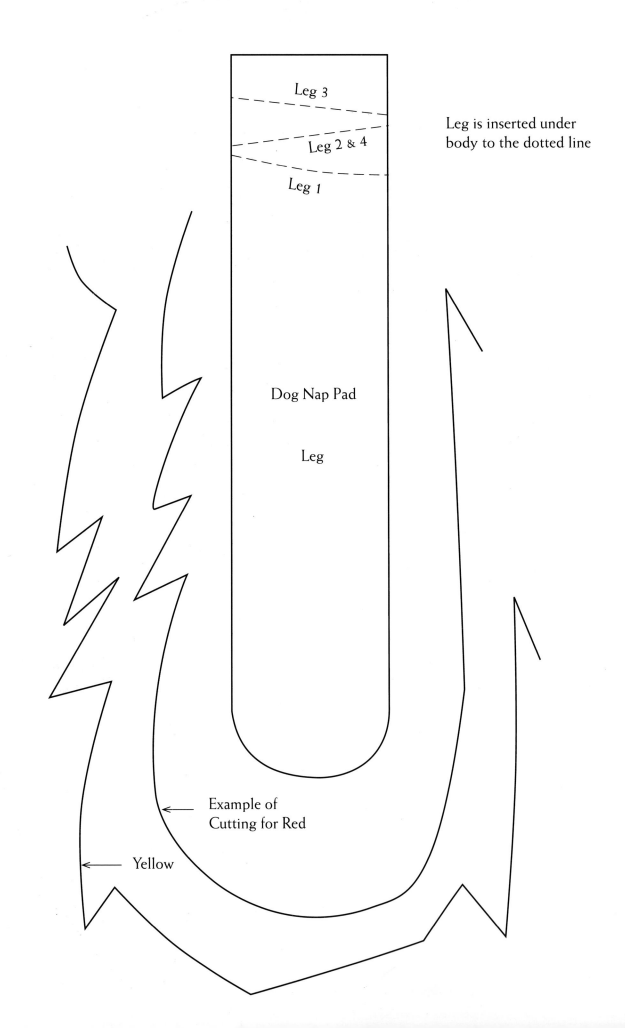

Leg 3

Leg 2 & 4

Leg 1

Leg is inserted under
body to the dotted line

Dog Nap Pad

Leg

Example of
Cutting for Red

Yellow

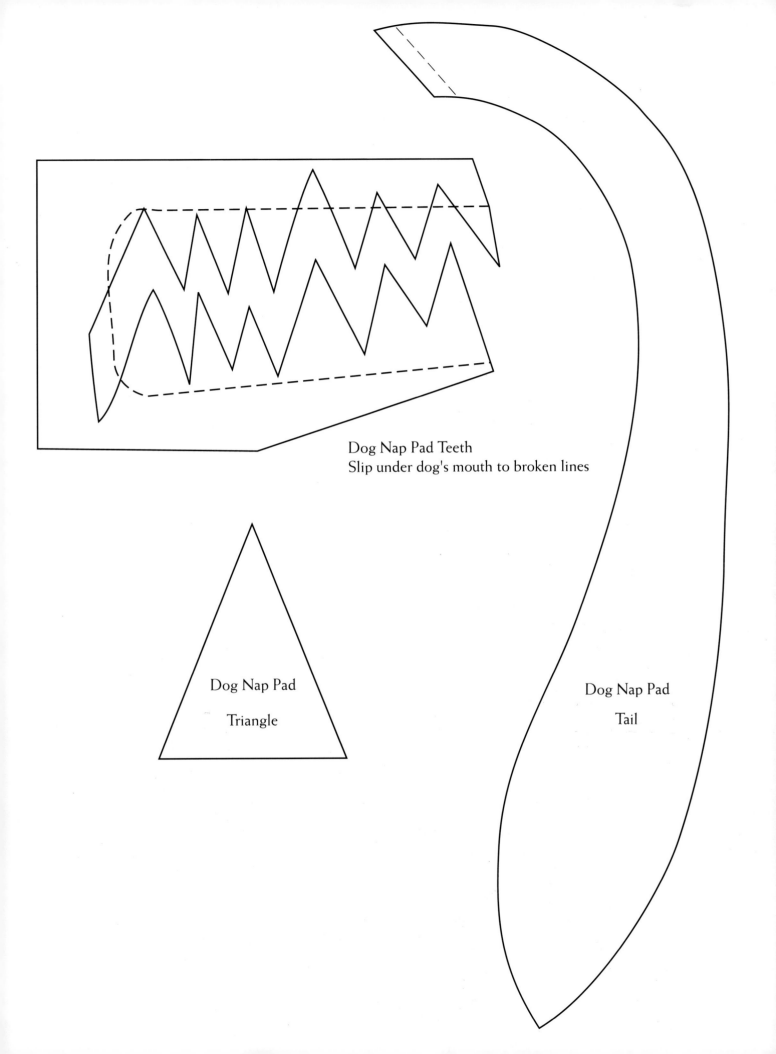

Dog Nap Pad Teeth
Slip under dog's mouth to broken lines

Dog Nap Pad

Triangle

Dog Nap Pad

Tail

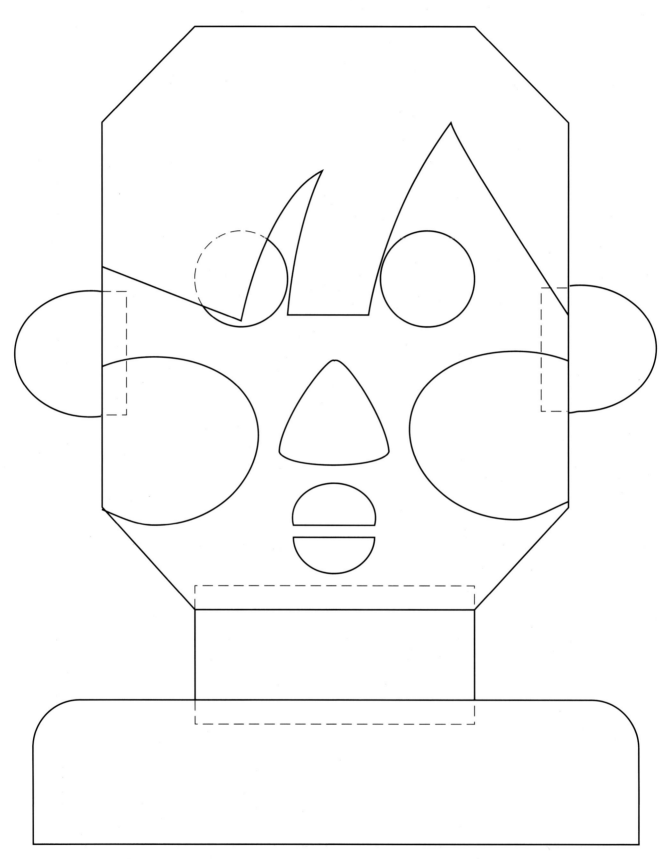

My Family Row 1–1

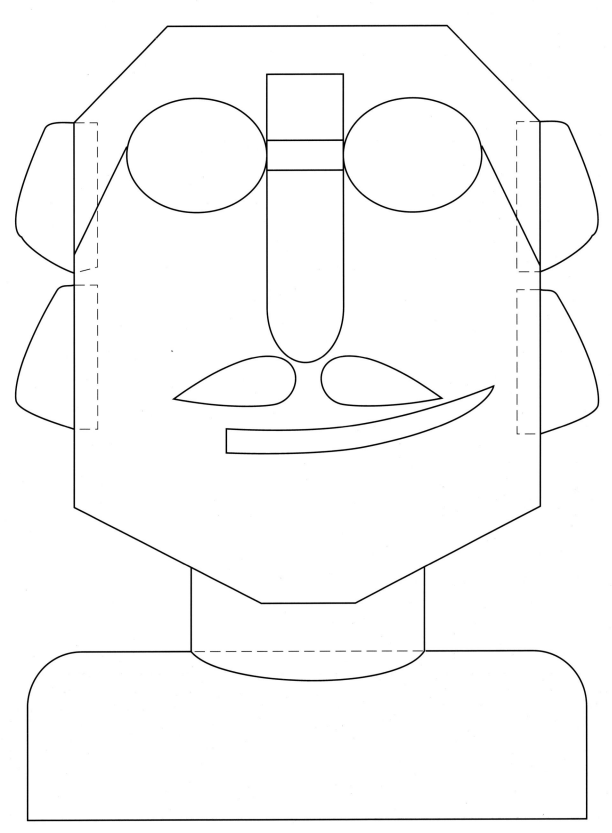

My Family Row 1–4

My Family Row 2–1

My Family Row 2–2

My Family Row 2–3

My Family Row 2–4

My Family Row 3–1

My Family Row 3–2

My Family Row 3–3

My Family Row 3–4

My Family Row 4–1

My Family Row 4–2

My Family Row 4–3

My Family Row 4–4

My Family Row 5–1

My Family Row 5–2

My Family Row 5–3

My Family Row 5—4

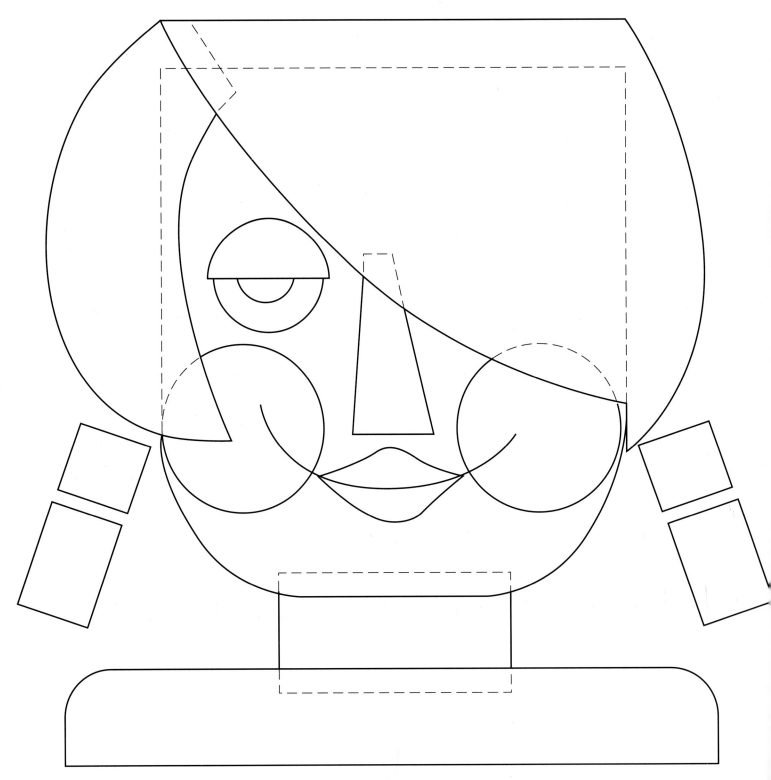

My Family Row 6–1

My Family Row 6–2

My Family Row 6–3

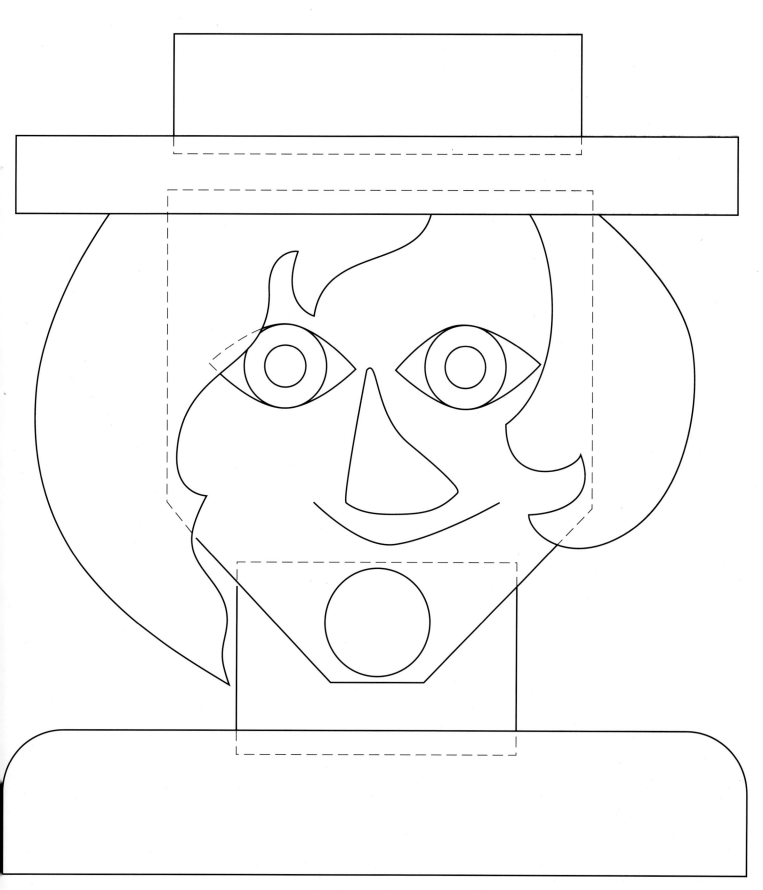

My Family Row 6–4

My Family Letters

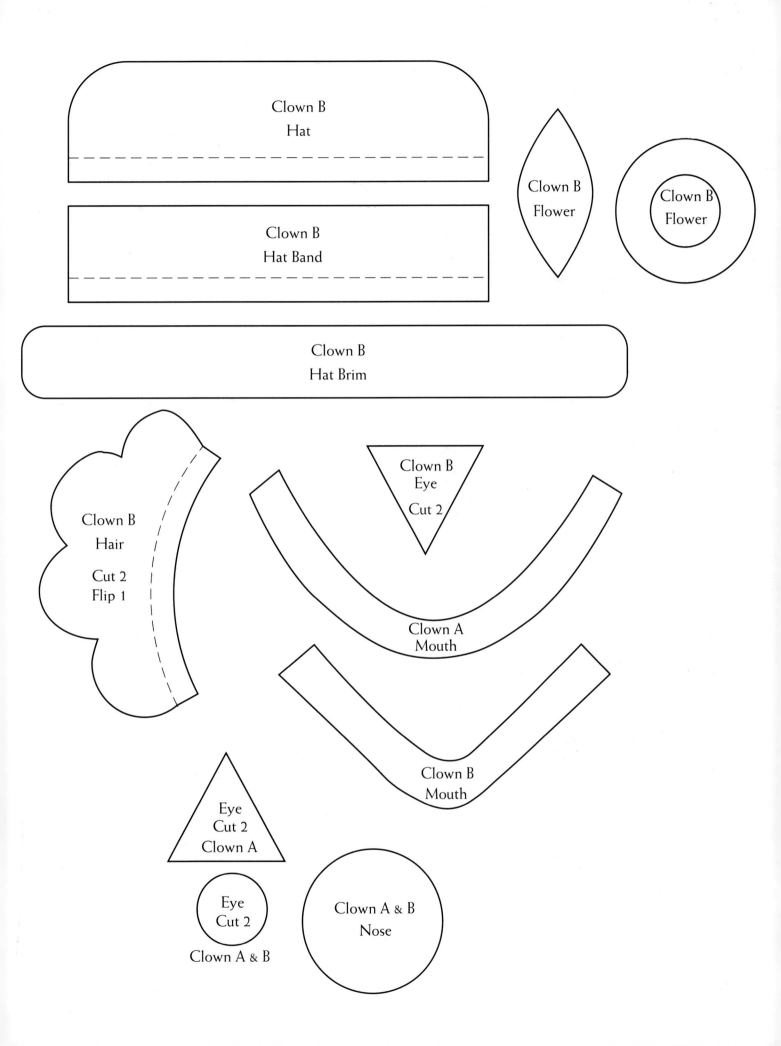

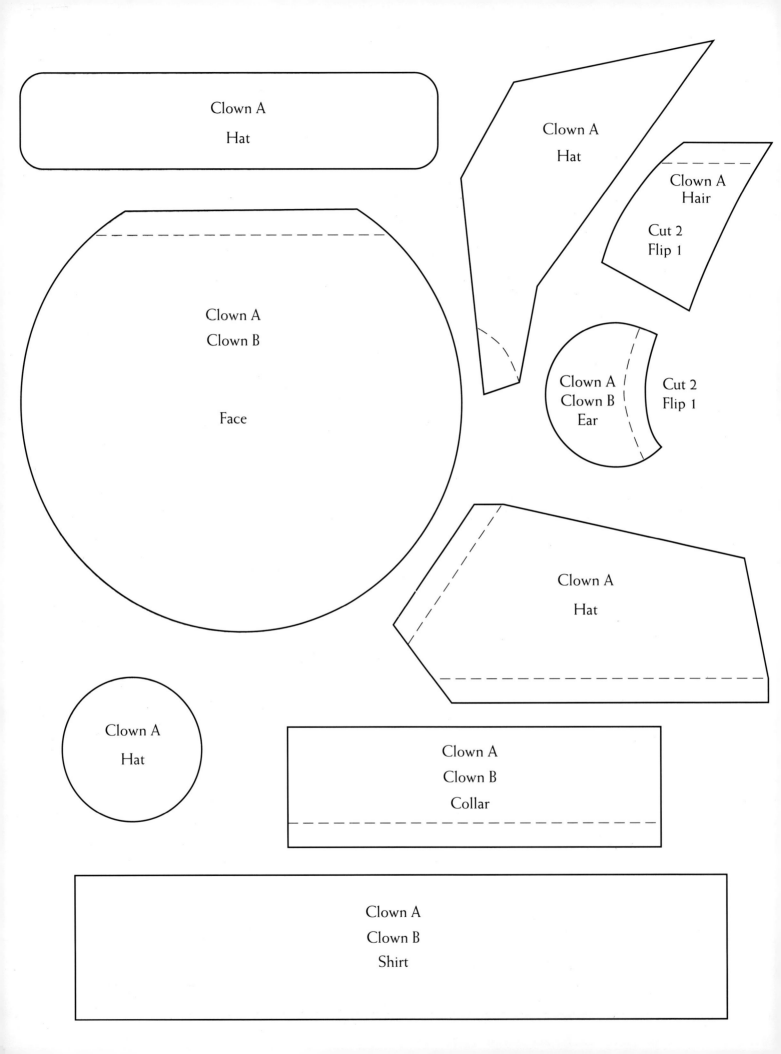

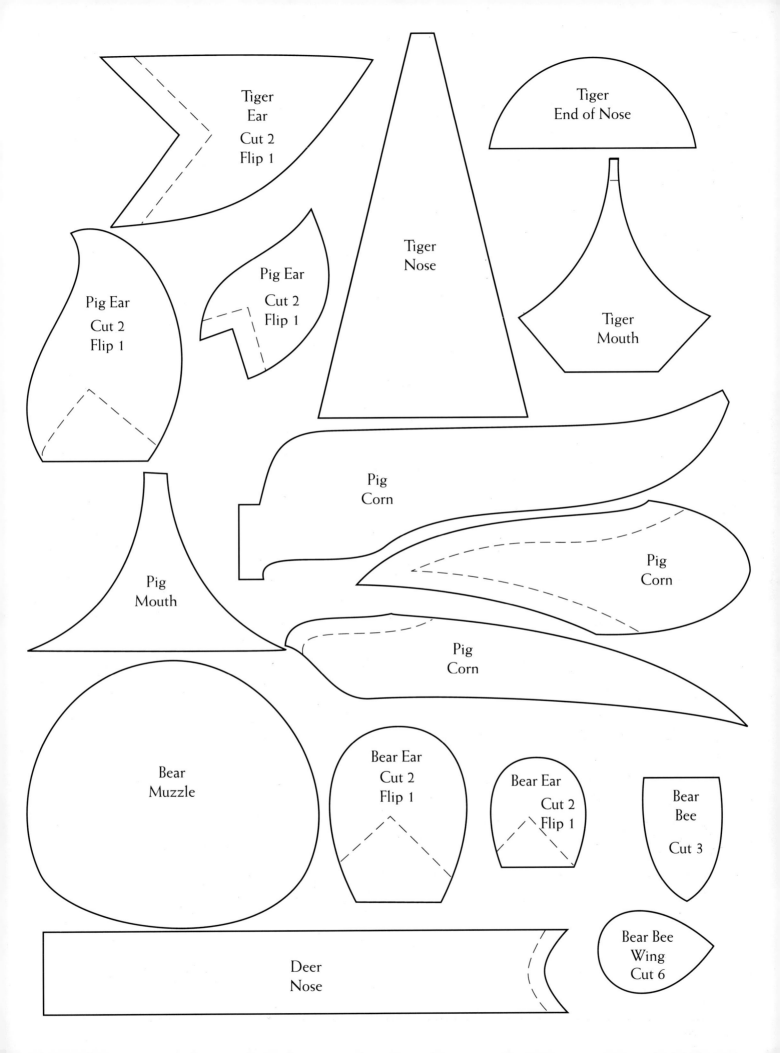

Tiger
Ear
Cut 2
Flip 1

Tiger
End of Nose

Pig Ear
Cut 2
Flip 1

Pig Ear
Cut 2
Flip 1

Tiger
Nose

Tiger
Mouth

Pig
Corn

Pig
Mouth

Pig
Corn

Pig
Corn

Bear
Muzzle

Bear Ear
Cut 2
Flip 1

Bear Ear
Cut 2
Flip 1

Bear
Bee
Cut 3

Bear Bee
Wing
Cut 6

Deer
Nose

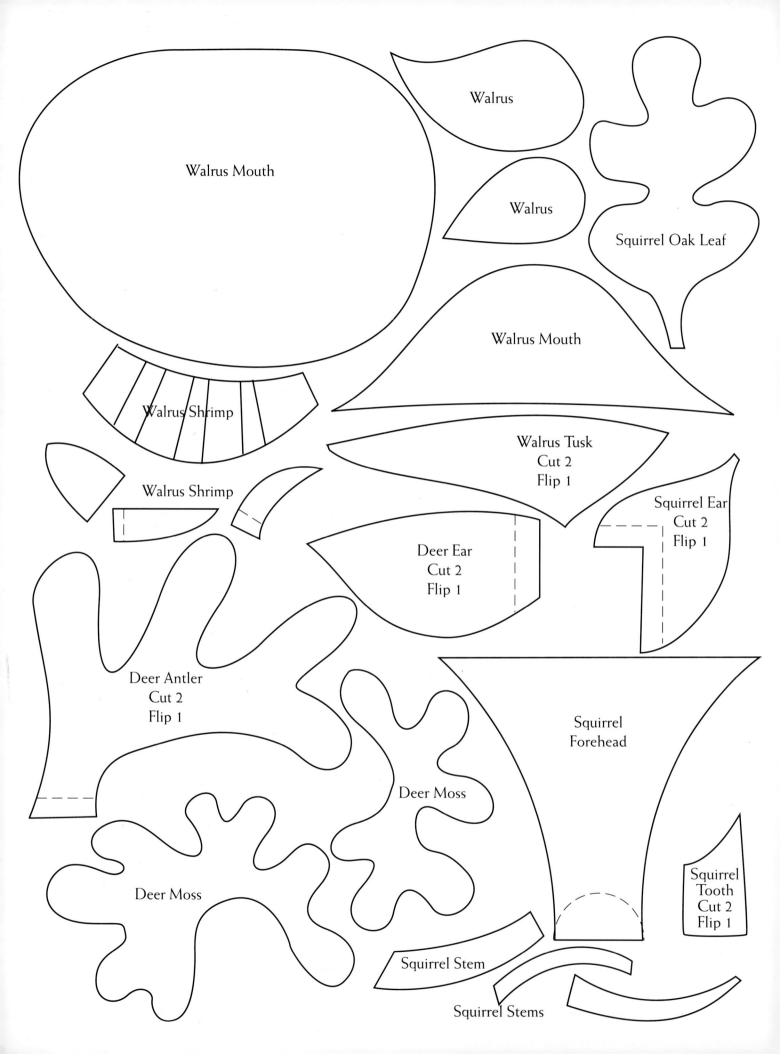

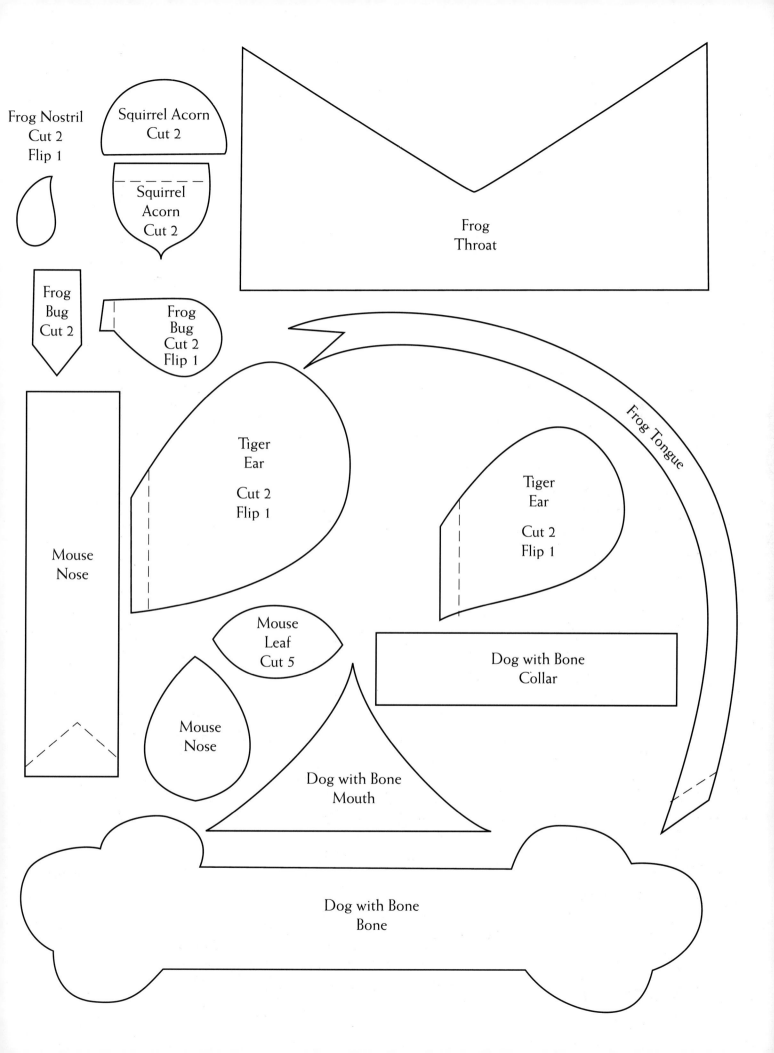

Frog Nostril
Cut 2
Flip 1

Squirrel Acorn
Cut 2

Squirrel
Acorn
Cut 2

Frog
Throat

Frog
Bug
Cut 2

Frog
Bug
Cut 2
Flip 1

Tiger
Ear
Cut 2
Flip 1

Tiger
Ear
Cut 2
Flip 1

Frog Tongue

Mouse
Nose

Mouse
Leaf
Cut 5

Dog with Bone
Collar

Mouse
Nose

Dog with Bone
Mouth

Dog with Bone
Bone

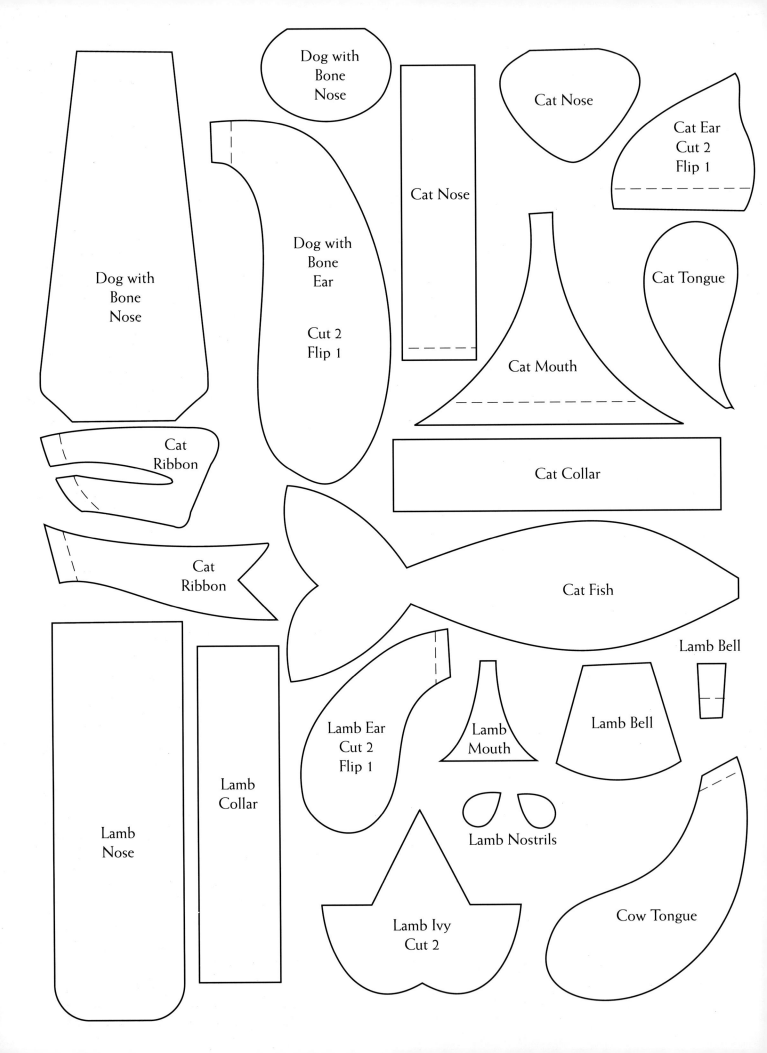

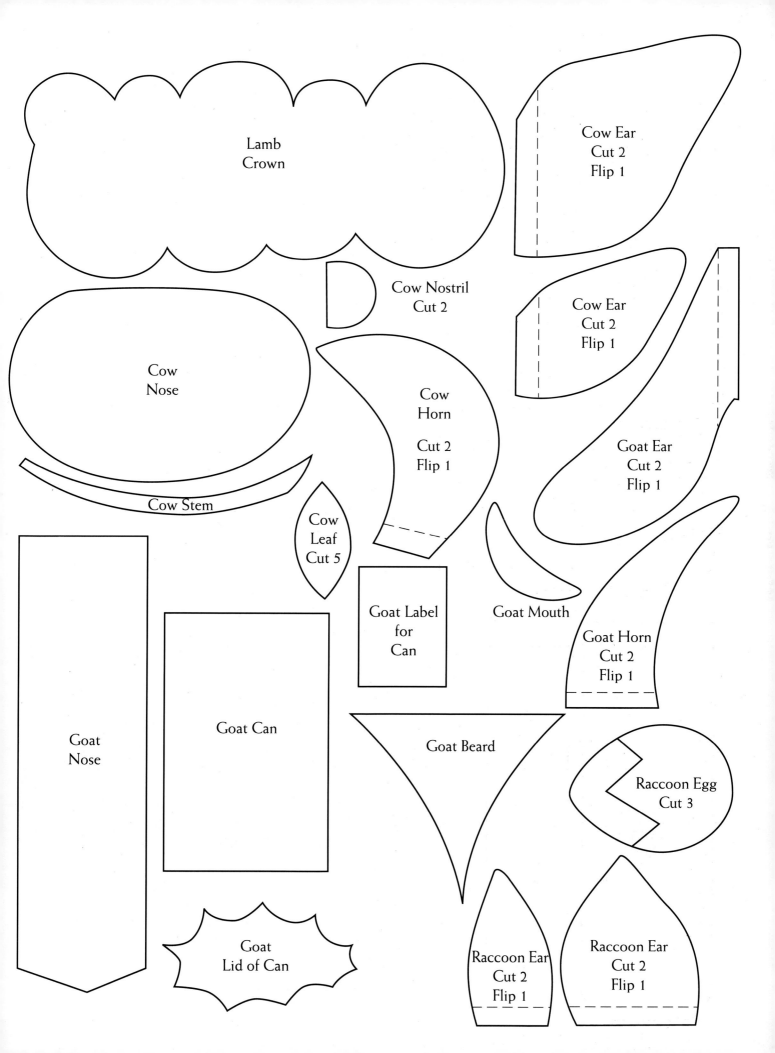

Lamb
Crown

Cow Ear
Cut 2
Flip 1

Cow Nostril
Cut 2

Cow Ear
Cut 2
Flip 1

Cow
Nose

Cow
Horn
Cut 2
Flip 1

Goat Ear
Cut 2
Flip 1

Cow Stem

Cow
Leaf
Cut 5

Goat Mouth

Goat Label
for
Can

Goat Horn
Cut 2
Flip 1

Goat
Nose

Goat Can

Goat Beard

Raccoon Egg
Cut 3

Goat
Lid of Can

Raccoon Ear
Cut 2
Flip 1

Raccoon Ear
Cut 2
Flip 1

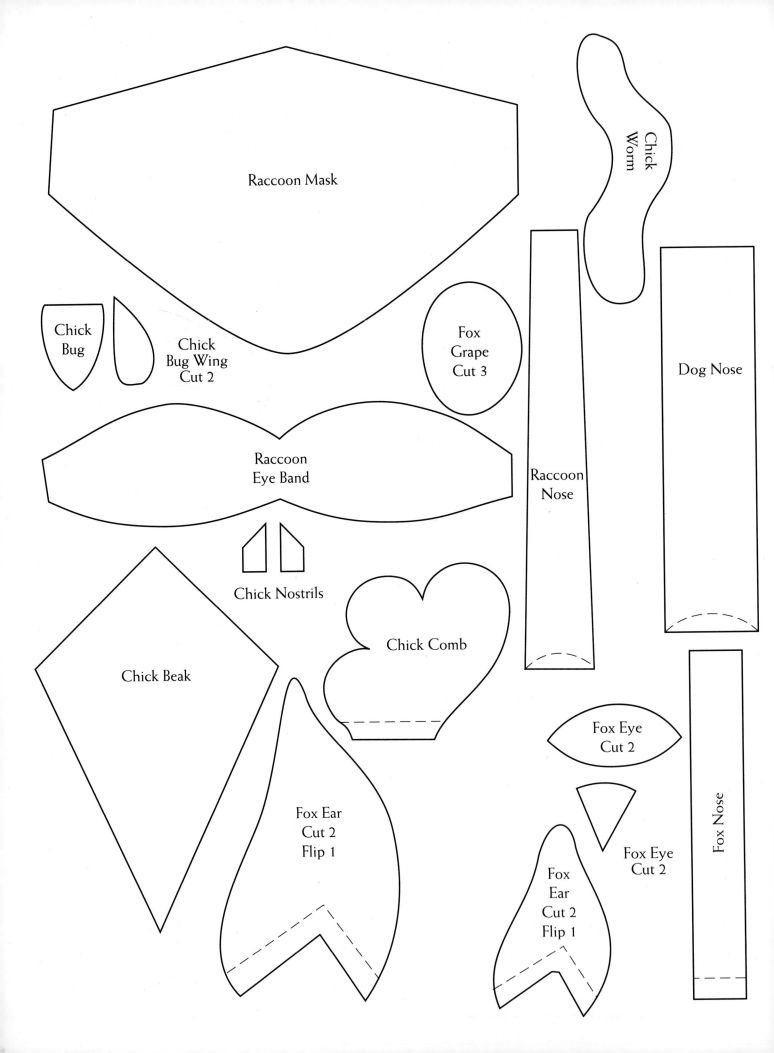

Raccoon Mask

Chick Worm

Chick Bug

Chick Bug Wing Cut 2

Fox Grape Cut 3

Dog Nose

Raccoon Eye Band

Raccoon Nose

Chick Nostrils

Chick Comb

Chick Beak

Fox Eye Cut 2

Fox Ear Cut 2 Flip 1

Fox Eye Cut 2

Fox Nose

Fox Ear Cut 2 Flip 1

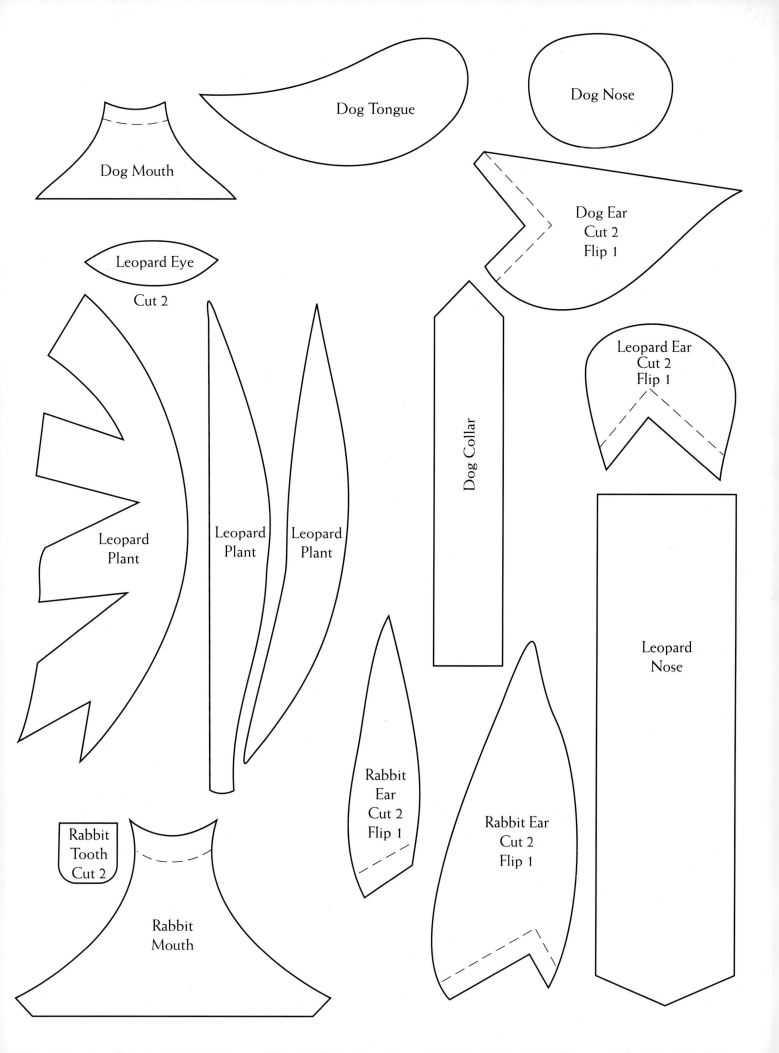

Dog Tongue

Dog Nose

Dog Mouth

Dog Ear
Cut 2
Flip 1

Leopard Eye
Cut 2

Leopard Ear
Cut 2
Flip 1

Leopard
Plant

Leopard
Plant

Leopard
Plant

Dog Collar

Leopard
Nose

Rabbit
Ear
Cut 2
Flip 1

Rabbit Ear
Cut 2
Flip 1

Rabbit
Tooth
Cut 2

Rabbit
Mouth

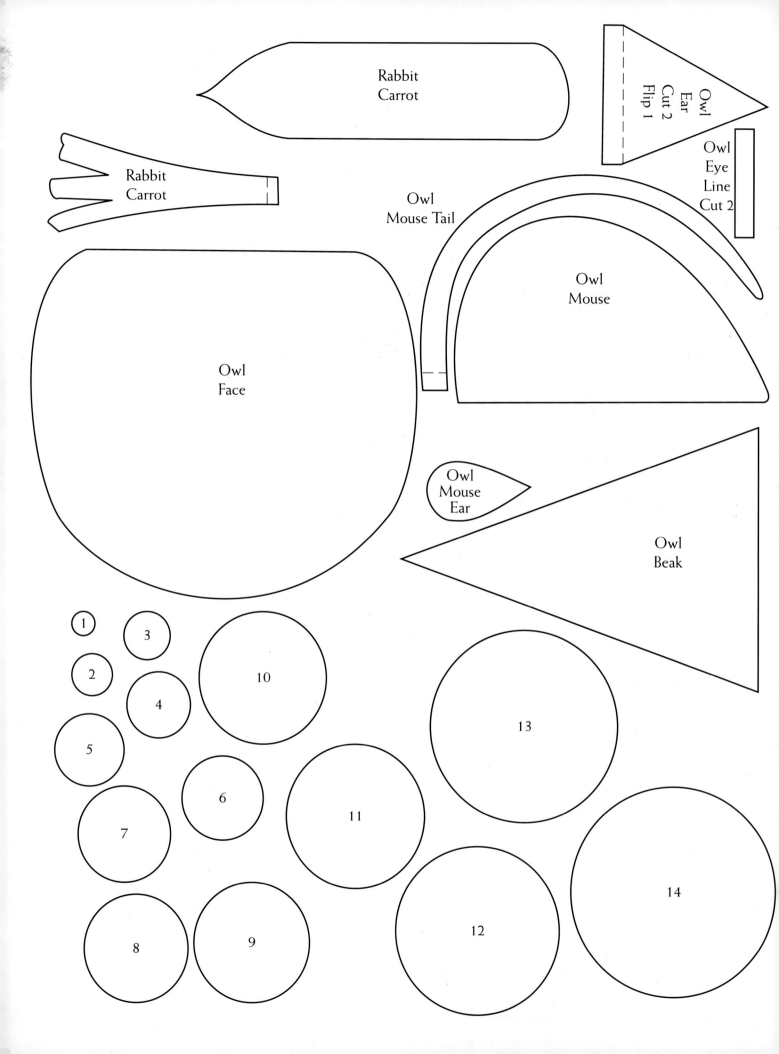

Rabbit
Carrot

Owl
Ear
Cut 2
Flip 1

Owl
Eye
Line
Cut 2

Rabbit
Carrot

Owl
Mouse Tail

Owl
Mouse

Owl
Face

Owl
Mouse
Ear

Owl
Beak

1
2
3
4
5
6
7
8
9
10
11
12
13
14